1.95

Wait Without Idols

❋❋❋❋❋❋❋❋❋❋❋❋❋❋❋❋❋❋❋❋❋❋❋❋

BY GABRIEL VAHANIAN

The Death of God

WAIT
WITHOUT
IDOLS

✳✳✳✳✳✳✳✳✳✳✳✳✳✳✳✳✳✳✳✳✳✳✳✳

GABRIEL VAHANIAN

GEORGE BRAZILLER

NEW YORK

À MA MÈRE
qui m'a appris à lire
ce qu'on peut lire dans tous les livres
et dans aucun

Library of Congress Catalog Card Number: 64-11429

Second Printing

PRINTED IN THE UNITED STATES OF AMERICA

Preface

****

From the time of St. Augustine to the present, Western literature is *christian** literature. This is true whether it represents an adequate or merely a superficial artistic transcription of the cultural significance of the Christian faith. It is also, and perhaps especially, true when it represents modern man's growing disillusionment with the

---

* The distinction between Christian (with a capital *C*) and *christian* (small *c*)—which we have italicized in the Preface to avoid confusion—simply serves to introduce the idea that the literature of the West, whether or not it conforms with Christianity, presupposes a cultural context informed and shaped by Christianity. This distinction and its applications are also valid in other domains than that of literature. We consider as *christian* not only that which participates in the cultural vocation of Christianity, but also that which deviates from it, or, in terms of a religious or ideological allegiance, even seems to contradict it.

Christian tradition. Neither *The Brothers Karamazov* nor *The Sound and the Fury*, any less than the *Confessions*, can be properly understood apart from an intimate knowledge of that faith and tradition.

The same thing applies, or applies at least in part, to the literature of our post-Christian age, insofar as it continues the cultural tradition of the Christian era. Other philosophies or ideologies may have supplanted Christianity in providing a matrix for the creative imagination, but the cultural framework of such imagination is nonetheless originally determined and shaped by that tradition. Thus, when a contemporary novelist puts into question the reality of God, or excludes it from the world of his fiction, the fact that it is the cultural reality of the God of the Christian tradition that he rejects allows us, if not directly to qualify his work as *christian*, at least to apply to it without violating its integrity the principles of a *christian* literary criticism.

The meaning and purpose of such criticism are not determined by any surreptitious design to Christianize everything that is written. Our purpose in the present book is rather to probe into the human situation of post-Christian man, to elicit from it the shape of his ultimate concern and express the nature of the question that every man is unto himself, whether or not God is the answer, and whether or not it presupposes or leads to the question of God.

Nor has this anything to do with the author's or the reader's commitment to Christianity, or their denial of its validity. At the risk of offending the professional Christian, let us state at the outset that a literary work of art is made susceptible to a legitimate *christian* interpretation simply by its literary qualities, and not by its ostensibly apologetic compliance with the pseudomorality of religious standards of conduct. The *christian* or even occasionally Christian quality of Western literature is determined by the same aesthetic standards by which any novel or play or poem is singled out as a signal witness to man's creative imagination.

We do not imply, of course, that aesthetic and religious standards are synonymous, although there is obviously a kinship that mutually affects the destinies of art and religion. In many respects the gap between art or literature and the Christian tradition has been reduced, thanks especially to the undisputed excellence of some of our major novelists and poets, playwrights, filmmakers, and painters. But what captures the imagination is the growing denunciation of the insufficiencies of the Christian tradition in coping with the situation of modern man. This is why we feel there is something incongruous when Matisse "steps out" of himself to design a Christian chapel, until we realize that the genius of Matisse consisted precisely in his ability to help us to overcome this feeling of incongruity. There is no discrepancy between his art and the Christian verities enshrined in or witnessed to by such a chapel.

Efforts like this, however, are exceptional. On the whole, modern art and in particular modern literature have increasingly tended to give us the impression that religion is a special domain that, for all practical purposes, is severed from the everyday and the real, from daily existence. The reason is largely that the religious symbols that are capable of a genuine literary expression have lost their immediate cultural significance. Neither these symbols nor their cultural relevance is readily accessible to us.

But we are so inclined by nature that we still hunger for such symbols. Otherwise, we should not understand the delayed success of William Golding's *Lord of the Flies*, and the incongruous hunt for symbols that he triggered by his disclosure that the novel was symbolic through and through. And yet, despite the artificiality of such an undertaking, even Golding's work serves to illustrate our basic contention that the infrastructure of the creative imagination, by which Western man projects his self-understanding and recognizes himself, has been shaped by the influence of the Christian tradition. Nothing else is meant when we claim that the principles of a *christian* literary criticism are naturally germane to an existential exegesis of Western literature.

Three theses enable us to formulate the principal expressions of this basic assumption, and constitute the point of view from which the following essays are composed. Although these theses seem to be cast in theological language, their validity depends on their relevance to the works of literature we have selected for analysis.

We shall try to show that our guiding principle never is imported from theology into literature; we do not intend to annex literature by arbitrarily "baptizing" it into Christianity. Nor do we by any means imply that Christianity is the only answer to the questions raised in the course of our analysis, and on the sole basis of the texts under consideration. Such an approach to literature, often adopted by Christian commentators, is dishonest and cannot be qualified otherwise than as a fraud. Sartre did not write *No Exit* so that a Christian would use it as a homiletic pretext for all kinds of easy and cheap considerations about the situation of man without God. Our approach is diametrically opposed to this kind of abusive and *pro domo* interpretation to which literature is fallaciously subjected by those whose concern is merely a utilitarian apology of an etiolated Christianity.

The first thesis is that what makes the religious tradition of Western culture is also what accounts for the *christian* quality of our literary tradition. Not that either tradition is to be assimilated with or subjected to the other, or that there must be a strict correspondence between them. Indeed, today they would seem to be so disconnected as to belie our contention. But we must not be misled by this superficial disparateness. What we have in mind is something like what obtained during the Puritan period, when, as Tillich puts it, the civil community, symbolized by the Town Hall, and the Christian community, symbolized by the Church, were one and the same community grounded in the same principle—the

Word of God—and guided by a common allegiance to the very Word of God by which they yet were constituted differently.[1] However, this same principle, which at first only sanctioned a formal distinction between Church and State, subsequently gave birth to the notion of their necessary separation. *Mutatis mutandis*, the rise of secularism drove a wedge between religion and culture; and their separation need not have become so detrimental to either had Christianity not forfeited its cultural responsibility and become so tradition-bound as to seem today more "tradition" than Christian.

Our second thesis is that both literature and the Christian tradition, at least in its primitive and essential thrust, are iconoclastic. What is meant by this term is defined and, we hope, sufficiently clarified in the introductory chapter. For the sake of convenience, let us state here that there are two kinds of iconoclasm: true and false. The Christian tradition, in its contemporary setting, has practically ceased to be iconoclastic in the true sense. As for literature, it is iconoclastic in both senses of the term. When it is truly so, our first thesis is by the same token vindicated. It is falsely iconoclastic when it appears to be violently opposed to the original principles of the Christian tradition and to the latter's fundamental notions about God, man, or Christ and his relevance to modern man's self-understanding. In either case, there seems to be no bridge between the transcendental universe of the Christian tradition and the immanentist

frame of reference in which modern man lives six days
out of seven.

And yet, good or bad, truly or falsely, literature is
today more iconoclastic than Christianity. The significance of this statement might be underlined by adding
that, true or false, iconoclasm is an attempt, not to re-
create, but to transfigure the world and man's situation
in it, including all the everyday aspects of existence. As
Erich Auerbach has amply shown in *Mimesis*,[2] the Christian tradition did once influence literature in this direction. However, we differ slightly in our terminology. Instead of Auerbach's "figura" and "figural," we prefer
the term "transfiguration" in order to stress the original
goodness of the world, of man, of the creation as a whole.
Besides, "figura" applies more aptly to a conception that
endows the universe with a definitely supernatural purpose, whereas the concept of "transfiguration" is more
meaningful in the context of the present *Zeitgeist*, which
is predicated on the irrelevance of God if he exists, and
proclaims the purposelessness of the world and the
"tragic *nonsense* of life."

As for the third thesis, it may be stated by saying that
the line of demarcation between God and the idol is a
thin one. Rationally, God cannot be distinguished from
the idol, just as in theological language we would affirm
that the believer is not justified by his faith. From this
it follows that idolatry is but a caricature of faith in
God and that, similarly, man often is but a caricature of
himself, even to the extent of being nothing other than

such a caricature. It also follows that today, more than ever before, there is no merit in being a Christian; that is to say, being a Christian is unmerited.

The conclusion brought to light by these essays in literary criticism is that in the biblical conception of God, the reality of God is ever independent of the cultural frame in which it may be grasped. In other words, our conception of God need not conform with the biblical concept, externally. The Bible speaks of God in terms of a world view to which it also adheres in other respects. It is consistent with itself. Surely, the least that must be expected from contemporary Christianity is an equal amount of self-consistency. Likewise, the biblical understanding of Christ's person and his work is dependent upon the contemporaneous world view and its cultural setting. The events of Christ's life make this dependence quite plain. But it is equally plain that the presentness of God to man (that is, the incarnation) and the possibility of authentic existence, except conceptually, do not ultimately depend upon man's world view, whether it is mythological or scientific.

It is in this light that we hope to have justified the three groups of essays that constitute the main body of this book. In the first group, we have included Hawthorne, Melville, and Faulkner, partly because their spiritual kinship is fairly obvious and partly because all three are American; the influence of the American novel (and of Faulkner in particular) on the international scene has far exceeded that of the novel of any other country in our century. Apart from this, Hawthorne shows how the Christian tradition is losing its iconoclastic task, whereas Melville seems to construe literature as essentially such a task, and Faulkner is concerned with transfiguring the world in an authentically iconoclastic way.

In the second group, Eliot fails to awaken poetry to its ultimate vocation and becomes tradition-bound; Auden shows how only the iconoclast can transfigure the world; and from Perse we learn how the world can be transfigured without relying upon the iconoclasm of the Christian tradition, since we live in a post-Christian era.

In the third group, Dostoevski unmasks the false pretenses of inauthentic iconoclasm; Lagerkvist is torn between faith and unfaith; while Kafka both sheds a tortured light on a quest into which he lures us for an *introuvable* God and shows how our concept of God need not be subservient to the cultural exigencies of any previous world, including that of the Bible.

Though each essay may be read separately—and for this reason some repetition has been found necessary—the reader will be aware of the progression of thought that our analysis effects from one study to the next and from one group to the other. The repetition and the variations of our central motif, as in a musical composition, are the integrating factor of these studies. Our sole purpose has been to illustrate the significance of theological insights into the nature of man and their rich relevance to an investigation of the domain of literature. And our hope is that these essays in *christian* literary criticism may partly exonerate theology from its cultural ineptitude and partly redeem literary criticism from the vacuous purpose to which it often seems to delight in condemning itself.

—GABRIEL VAHANIAN

June 1963

Acknowledgments

****

THE following material has been slightly altered and incorporated into this book: "The Lost Iconoclasm of Christianity," published in *The Nation* (April 22, 1961); "Beyond the Death of God: the need of cultural revolution," published in *Dialog* (Autumn 1962); and "Pär Lagerkvist," published in *Ararat* (Winter 1962). I wish to thank the respective editors of these magazines for permission to make use again of these articles.

I also wish to acknowledge gratefully the kindness of the following publishers for the permission to quote from certain works studied in this book:

The Bollingen Foundation—for selections from *Exile and Other Poems, Eloges and Other Poems,* and *Winds* by Saint-John Perse, published by Pantheon Books, Inc.;

Harcourt, Brace & World, Inc.—from "The Waste Land," "Choruses from 'The Rock,' " "Ash Wednesday," and "Journey of the Magi" in *Collected Poems 1909–1962* by T. S. Eliot, copyright, 1936, by Harcourt, Brace & World, Inc.; © 1963, 1964, by T. S. Eliot; and from "East Coker" in *Four Quartets*, copyright 1943, by T. S. Eliot. Reprinted by permission of Harcourt, Brace & World, Inc.;

Random House, Inc.—from "Prime" (*Nones*), reprinted from *The Shield of Achilles*, by W. H. Auden, by permission of Random House, Inc., copyright 1951 by W. H. Auden; from *The Age of Anxiety*, by W. H. Auden, copyright 1946, 1947 by W. H. Auden, reprinted by permission of Random House, Inc.; and from "As I Walked out one evening" (*Another Time*), copyright 1940 by W. H. Auden, and from "For the Time Being," copyright 1944 by W. H. Auden, reprinted from *The Collected Poetry of W. H. Auden*, by permission of Random House, Inc.

Finally, I owe a special debt of gratitude to Mr. Edwin Seaver for his encouraging suggestions and corrections and for his helpful criticism, as a result of which this book has come closer to attaining the goal I had set for myself in anticipation of the reader's indulgence.

—GABRIEL VAHANIAN

Contents

✳✳✳✳✳✳✳✳✳✳✳✳✳✳✳✳✳✳✳✳✳✳✳✳✳✳✳✳✳✳✳✳✳✳

How can his knowledge protect his desire for truth from illusion? How can he wait without idols to worship. . . ?

—W. H. AUDEN

I.
Iconoclasm and Transfiguration

✳✳✳✳✳✳✳✳✳✳✳✳✳✳✳✳✳✳✳✳✳✳✳✳✳✳✳

Man is the image and glory of God.

Now the Lord is the Spirit; and where the Spirit of the Lord is, there is liberty. And because for us there is no veil over the face, we all reflect as in a mirror the splendour of the Lord; thus we are transfigured into his likeness, from splendour to splendour; such is the influence of the Lord who is Spirit.

—Saint Paul[1]

Christianity as Iconoclasm

✳✳✳✳✳✳✳✳✳✳✳✳✳✳✳✳✳✳✳✳✳✳✳✳✳

THE history of religion is the history of spiritual degeneration. Every fragment of evidence tends to support this view. At the same time, no one would hesitate to agree with the anthropologist or the cultural historian that religious beliefs have on the whole become less and less barbaric, and religious practices and institutions more and more civilizing as well as civilized. As such, whatever one wishes to say about religion, positive or negative, one must define it as man's attempt to cover up his sense of shame. The Swiss Pestalozzi[1] and the contemporary theologian Wilhelm Vischer[2] have already said this. But what they have left unsaid is the direct relation between this sense of shame, spiritual degeneration and iconoclasm.

Religion degenerates into a sense of shame as soon

as it ceases to be iconoclastic. Whether this statement can be made about all religions is beyond our present scope. It certainly applies to the Christian tradition, and is relevant to an understanding of the failure of nerve characteristic of the contemporary religious climate. This failure is derived primarily from the fact that Christianity has forfeited its essentially iconoclastic responsibility; and consequently other movements, other ideologies have assumed—one might say usurped—this fundamentally monotheistic function, to the extent that the very meaning of iconoclasm has been altered. It is this alteration of the term, as well as the human reality it reveals, that is deadly to the spiritual and cultural implications of faith in a transcendent God, as presented in biblical thought. Christianity seems altogether unconcerned about this—which it would not be if it were still iconoclastic in the biblical sense.

Indeed, the biblical sense of the term differs greatly from its modern meaning. In common usage, iconoclasm refers today, according to the Oxford dictionary, to "the breaking or destroying of images; especially, of images and pictures set up as objects of veneration." This definition includes attitudes reflecting the whole range from the Mosaic prohibition of graven images to the antireligious acts of totalitarianism and libertarianism alike, by way of the puritanical distrust of the senses common to Judaism and Islam as well as Christianity. Basically, however, the contemporary meaning of iconoclasm is related to two distinct attitudes: on the one hand, the anti-artistic drive of both Catholic and Protestant puritanism; on the other hand, the Promethean or blasphemous revolts against the monotheism of the Christian tradition. The first of these attitudes was typified by André Gide when he remembered that, because of his puritan upbringing, for a long time he had represented "the Protestant, the anti-artist, the enemy."[3] An example of the second attitude may be found in Baudelaire, who exclaimed: "Peter denied his Master? . . . He did right!"[4] For Baudelaire considered that love is as "august" a religion as any, especially when it vindicates man. Thus he wrote:

> Which of the gods will dare thy judge to be,
> And to condemn thy brow with labour pale,
> Not having balanced in his golden scale
> The flood of tears thy brooks poured in the sea?
> Which of the gods will dare thy judge to be?
>
> What boot the laws of just and of unjust?[5]

We cannot here establish whether there is a connection between the puritan and Promethean versions of iconoclasm, without being drawn into an intricate theological subject; or trace the possible relation between either iconoclasm and the radical iconoclasm of biblical thought. We shall, instead, concern ourselves with the contention that the base itself of biblical thought consists of an unadulterated iconoclasm and that, by contrast, Christianity is *practically* no longer iconoclastic.

It is necessary, first, to clarify a fundamental divergence between the modern, *i.e.*, Promethean, and the biblical meaning of the term. Briefly, modern iconoclasm is an antidivine manifestation, whereas the biblical form is a deflation of man's natural inclination to deify himself, or his society, or the State, or his culture. In this light, any reader of the Bible will discern the relentless exposing of this manifold, constant proclivity to elevate the finite to the level of the infinite, to give to the transitory the status of the permanent, and to attribute to man qualities that will deceive him into denying his finitude. In short, biblical iconoclasm is directed against any latent or overt self-deification and against "ethnolatry" in any one of its forms: racial, national, cultural. Ethnolatry is the reduction of a particular civilization and the religion identifying it to the characteristics of a race and the idolization of its idiosyncrasy. Biblical iconoclasm is directed against man's most subtle and degenerate idol—himself. Whenever this is overlooked, the particularity of biblical thought is by the same token grievously bypassed.

This particularity can, indeed, be seen from the first to the last book of the Bible. The myths of man's creation in the image of God and of the Last Judgment are misunderstood when they are not grasped as implying a conception of man that is the direct antithesis to all sorts of human apotheoses. Unlike common sense, pretension to deity is equally distributed among men. But the biblical position is clear: man is not God and, especially, he may not pull divine rank on his fellowmen. For the same reasons, neither nature nor history, which has a beginning and an end, is endowed with divinity.

Similarly, the rejection of ethnolatry is unambiguously stated throughout the Bible. Perhaps the most explicit statement is to be found in the Prophets' exposé of the mass religiosity of their day: from being a chosen people, Israel had now come to the point where it conceived of itself as a nation choosing its own god, forgetting that it was God who chose Israel. The Prophets unmasked and condemned the ethnolatry that had paralyzed Israel (and will paralyze any nation). A similar condemnation of ethnolatry, though it may be implicit rather than explicit, is to be found in the New Testament myth of the incarnation and of the fulfillment of the messianic hope in and through Jesus. National messianism, of the type that, Christians claim, Jesus did not represent, is another variant of ethnolatry. Saint Paul himself was repudiating the last vestiges of ethnolatrous messianism when he contended that in his understanding of the incarnation "there is neither Greek nor Jew." And Paul implemented his opinion by arguing that pagan converts to Christianity need not be first circumcised, in accordance with Jewish law, to become full members of the Christian community.

We find the same anti-idolatrous strain in the works of Saint Augustine and Saint Thomas, Luther and Calvin. Varied and even conflicting as their respective positions may be, they have one thing in common: a loyalty to the principle that biblical faith is monotheistic and demands a correlatively radical opposition to all divinization of symbolic events or institutions as well as of man himself. "When the principle of being is God," writes Richard Niebuhr[6] in *Radical Monotheism and Western Culture*, "then He alone is holy and ultimate sacredness must be denied to any special being. No special places, times, persons, or communities are more representative of the One than any others are. No sacred groves or temples, no hallowed kings or priests, no festival days, no chosen communities are particularly representative of Him in whom all things live and move and have their being." Iconoclasm is, for all practical purposes, the essential ingredient of monotheism as understood in the biblical tradition. Without this element, faith in God loses its indispensable character, and can result neither in radical commitment to God nor in an equally radical and iconoclastic involvement in the world.

It was this *sine qua non* of the incipient Christian movement that struck a different note in the religiously saturated atmosphere of the Graeco-Roman world and appealed to those who sought a new allegiance and a new self-understanding. As a matter of fact, the Roman authorities at first declared that Christianity was an illicit religion precisely because, from their point of view, Christianity meant atheism. And the reason the early Christians were charged with atheism was that they obstinately refused to make room for the cult of the emperor in the order of their religious services (for on this basis alone could any religion be legally recognized). Christianity could not bow down to this decree of imperial deification, which was universally applied with one single exception: Judaism was exempted from honoring it.

Later on, Augustine became the iconoclastic critic of religious isolationism, of Christian ethnolatry. Similarly, Thomas Aquinas' reliance on Aristotle was in the thirteenth century no less than a repudiation of the intellectual isolationism that the Christian tradition was being tempted by. The iconoclasm of the Reformation is better known, for it has been made notorious. But we would be in error if we did not realize that the Reformers' iconoclasm was also and chiefly an instrument of combat against ecclesiastic pretension to deity, or simply to sacredness. And we should not hesitate to apprehend in the same light the better side of the iconoclasm that marks, or perhaps mars, the French Revolution. The latter is a monument to the iconoclastic rebellion against the claim of ecclesiastic sacredness, just as the American Revolution is a monument against the claim of theological sacredness. By the claim of ecclesiastical sacredness is meant the subjugation of cultural and social institutions to the usurpative authority of another institution, the Christian Church. The claim of theological sacredness refers to the authoritarian subordination of all institutions to the letter of a dead body of doctrines. The former is the Catholic (not necessarily

Roman), while the latter is the Protestant temptation of a religious absolutism that is fatal to the tradition of authentic Christian iconoclasm.

What has happened to this iconoclastic tradition? Has it exhausted itself? At any rate, it does not make itself felt and is no longer unambiguously active in the contemporary world. Its strength seems to have been drained, and with an exceptional voice heard now and then, here and there, *in deserto,* the Christian churches seem on the whole incapable of being seized with any kind of iconoclastic witness to the monotheistic faith they claim to profess. How does one explain this lethargy? Let us take an example.

Whatever part of our Western democratic ideals we owe to ancient Greece, our modern understanding of democracy makes no sense if we do not take into account the marks that the Christian tradition has left upon it. Just think of Jefferson's words, which every American knows by heart and which were given new meaning by Mr. Stevenson in the United Nations Security Council: "We hold these truths to be *self-evident,* that all men are *created* equal, that they are endowed by their *Creator* with certain inalienable rights." (Italics added.) Practically no one today sees any connection between such a statement and the meaning of the biblical notion according to which man is created in the image of God. On the contrary, the words "created" and "Creator" hardly shock us. They have lost their iconoclastic value.

Or consider democratic procedures in general. Reinhold Niebuhr, who suggests humility as the political cornerstone of democracy, defines the latter as "a method of finding proximate solutions for insoluble problems," and bases this method on the acknowledgment that "man's capacity for justice makes democracy possible; but man's inclination to injustice makes democracy necessary."[7] But it was W. H. Auden, a poet and not a theologian, who brought to light the iconoclastic element around which Niebuhr's paradoxes revolved. In his *New Year Letter* for 1940,[8] Auden wrote:

> . . . all that we can say
> Is: true democracy begins
> With free confession of our sins.
> In this alone are all the same,
> All are so weak that none dare claim
> "I have the right to govern," or
> "Behold in me the Moral Law."

Since "art is not life and cannot be / A midwife to society," it is questionable whether theological paradoxes and the Christian tradition can again play the rôle of "a midwife to society" as they once did when they were impelled by the force of their iconoclastic insights. For these insights have now become commonplace notions, not to say platitudes. Besides, what man in the street would ever connect checks and balances with the confessions of our sins? And while it may be true that no politician would point to himself as personifying the moral law, he most probably would not hesitate to confess the sins of his opponent. The point is this: the iconoclastic faith of the Christian tradition has, as in the time of the Prophets, fallen into an ethnolatric complacency. And the present degeneration of the Christian tradition is to be attributed to this loss of its iconoclastic nerve.

In this respect, our situation is similar to that of the Graeco-Roman world at the time of the birth of Christianity, except for the fact that the position of Christianity vis-à-vis the non-Christian religions has been reversed. The Greek gods had been discredited when the Christian God was ushered into the Western world. But what was true then is also true today: every religion degenerates when it discredits its god. And now as then, the mood is one of longing, such longing as is quenched only by an iconoclastic wind of the spirit. More and more evidently, Christianity is no longer moved by it; and our culture is expropriating Christianity. The Protestant churches—most of which owe their origins to social or ethnic differences—find it difficult to surmount the animosities of their ethnolatrous clannishness. And the Roman Catholics still wait for the Protestants to return and submit to Rome. A truly iconoclastic move would consist in the Protestant churches abdicating their individual infallibilities and in the Catholic Church abdicating its papal infallibility. But this would demand too much boldness from our comfortable, self-righteous, and degenerate religiosities.

The Need for a Cultural Revolution

****

OVER a century ago, Kierkegaard wrote in *Sickness Unto Death* that Christianity was "the fundamental misfortune of Christendom."[1] For a correct diagnosis of the contemporary situation, we need, it seems, simply reverse the terms and declare that "Christendom" is the fundamental misfortune of Christianity. Since the time of Kierkegaard the transition to the post-Christian era has, indeed, become an everyday reality, and the "death of God" is now the cultural "event" by which modern man recognizes and admits this change. More precisely, the "death of God" is, today, Western man's "confession" (in the sense of the French *aveu*), just as the triune God was once the symbol that inaugurated and sustained the Christian era of Western culture.

This does not mean, obviously, that God himself no

longer is but that, regardless of whether he is or not, his reality, as the Christian tradition has presented it, has become culturally irrelevant: God is *de trop*, as Sartre would say. Nor do we imply that the previous era was, theologically speaking, Christian and that ours is not. One thing is clear: not even the Christian era (inclusive of the highest stage of its development, wherever our theological preferences may locate it) ever quite fully bloomed into a golden age, or else Kierkegaard would not have come to his conclusion. We must, on the other hand, realize that Christianity did, during that period, body forth into "the historic reality of Christian culture" (to borrow the title of a disappointing book Professor Dawson has written on this subject).

Culturally—and this is the aspect that interests us here—there definitely was a Christian era. It may not have been perfect, especially from the theological point of view. It may even have rested on unsound scientific and philosophical premises. But its culture corresponded to its theology; and, more significantly, this correspondence, this congruence between theology and culture provided man with a system of values and a key to the understanding of his being, as well as giving a motif to his existence, to his work and his art, to his thinking. He understood in order to believe and he believed in order understanding of his being, as well as giving a motif to business of existing was also an act of faith. Not only theologically and philosophically, but culturally as well, the reality of God was taken for granted and was the starting point of both reflection and action.

No doubt it will be objected that this embellishes the past. Perhaps. It may even be that our theological systems are today more accurately biblical than those of scholasticism, whether Catholic or Protestant. To say the least, we have certainly developed a higher esteem of the dignity of man than was the case hitherto. And we have grown more refined—both in our instruments of civilization and in our cruelty. Today we act as if we had domesticated the earth and look forward to annexing the moon. But the crux of the matter lies elsewhere.

Once a no man's land, the world has now become a no God's land.

What this means is that the world has been deprived of its sacramental significance; human existence has lost its transcendental dimension. Shorn of its *sym-bolic* (*i.e.*, covenantal) significance, language still performs a duty as a means of communication, but it has been neutralized; communication does not necessarily entail, or presuppose, communion. In fact, human existence itself has been neutralized. We live in the latest fashion of the third person plural, in the world of the neutral, anonymous crowd. In other words, Christendom (and what else can this mean today but Western culture?) is the great misfortune of Christianity. And the situation would not be quite so ironical, were it not to Christianity itself that we owe this Western culture that has changed our world into a no God's land. Post-Christian man is the child of Christian man.

To avoid any possible misunderstanding, let us clarify

what we mean by "Christian man" and by "post-Christian" man.

In defining these categories we must particularly bear in mind that we are concerned with cultural realities rather than theological considerations. Our basic contention is that the primary difference between Christian man and post-Christian man is a cultural one. What distinguishes them is the cultural re-orientation of the latter and only secondarily the desuetude of the former's theological concern. An irreducible distance separates the cultural context of post-Christian man, and its latent religious concern, from the theological background of Christian man's cultural situation.

For example, according to Bultmann's[2] broad generalization, the Christian world view is mythological, ours is "scientific." Having renounced the mythological world view, to what extent can we, if at all, accept the theological values it represented? Undoubtedly, between Christian man and post-Christian man a certain kinship continues to exist, and this we have already admitted. But the kinship is merely genealogical—a matter of pedigree, as it were, intellectual, cultural, social, etc. The cold fact is that like de Gaulle's *Algérie de papa*, the Christianity of "papa" has also outlived its day. A new cultural context has been taking shape, which is putting into question not only the structures of Western civilization in its secular aspects, but also, and more importantly, its theological foundations, the religious tradition incarnated in these cultural structures.

Take another example. When the Renaissance human-
ists revived Greek culture, it evidently represented to
them something other than what it actually was, if only
because their world view had been affected by the Christian tradition. Likewise, it is no less certain that the
Greek tragedies have a different meaning for us, for
the simple reason that our sense of the tragic is not informed by the same beliefs: we do not believe in the
Greek gods. That is to say, we do not rely on the same
presuppositions, we do not make the same assumption,
we do not enter their world with the same world view.
Similar observations can no doubt be made about our
approach to other ancient religions or to contemporary
non-Western religions.

The respective points of view of post-Christian man
and Christian man are so radically different that the
former, looking at the Christian religion, can neither
accept it nor appropriate its values. Not that Christian
man was in any way less in need of God's grace than is
post-Christian man. As Saint Paul said, in a statement
which had theological validity alone, there is neither
Jew nor Greek; so also there is neither Christian man
nor post-Christian man. But Paul was doubtless aware
that between Jew and Greek one could sense a certain
cultural difference; it is, we contend, an even greater one
that distinguishes the Christian from post-Christian
man, between whom lies, like a continental divide, what
we call the death of God. The death of God is a cultural
phenomenon, expressive of the simplest fact that God

is no longer necessary and that his reality cannot be taken for granted.

The real problem, however, is even more complicated. It is easy to talk about God in a supernatural context, when human nature is understood in terms of a transcendental universe. But how can one speak of a transcendental God when only an immanentist frame of reference is available, and man construes both his situation in the world and the universe in immanentist concepts? It would be like translating the Bible into a language that has no word for God. (Just consider, incidentally, the traditional methods of apologetics. What rôle can apologetics play today in confronting the non-Christian? None, as long as the best we can do is to compare religions, although this perhaps is for the better if it forces Christian theology to become honest again and to content itself simply with being kerygmatic. Otherwise apologetics only helps us to make converts from other Christian denominations.)

At the risk of repeating ourselves, let us state clearly that what separates Christian man from post-Christian man is something of an entirely different nature from what distinguishes medieval man from modern man. We should find a better analogy in reflecting upon what separates pre-Christian man from Christian man. Like the early Christian, the post-Christian is ushering in a new era; but the charge of atheism that was leveled at the former is now welcomed by the latter. Post-Christian man even claims atheism as the only guarantee of a free and responsible action, as his existential presupposition and the act of his emancipation.

It is important to note that post-Christian man is not necessarily anti-Christian, or even non-Christian, inasmuch as, relatively speaking, he is the heir of the Christian tradition. The prefix "post" implies in the last analysis that any Western man is today post-Christian, even though he may still have faith in the transcending presence of God's reality as manifested in the Christ-event. Or else he is a vestigial Christian, who clings to superannuated forms of belief expressive of the cultural framework with which they once were congruous, even while otherwise sharing in the post-Christian mentality of his contemporaries.

Be that as it may, the fact remains that something has happened in the consciousness of Western man. This event may not have been recorded by theologians. But it has shaken the vision of poets and novelists, of artists and playwrights. On the one hand, the self-invalidation of the Christian tradition has been hailed as at last enabling man to face his condition with its attendant obligation to greatness and, equally, to assume the ambiguities of his self-understanding. On the other, the creative imagination has been frustrated or even betrayed by the secularism that has resulted from the expropriation of the Christian tradition. In the first category, one can cite Camus, Saint-John Perse, Beckett; the second includes Joyce, Eliot, Faulkner.

The following lines from T. S. Eliot's "The Rock"

quite appropriately describe the general characteristics
of this situation:

> But it seems that something has happened that has
>   never happened before: though we know not just
>   when, or why, or how, or where.
> Men have left GOD not for other gods, they say,
>   but for no god; and this has never happened
>   before.
> That men both deny god and worship gods, pro-
>   fessing first Reason,
> And then Money, and Power and what they call
>   Life, or Race, or Dialectic.
> The Church disowned, the tower overthrown, the
>   bells upturned, what have we to do
> But stand with empty hands and palms turned
>   upwards
> In an age which advances progressively back-
>   wards?[3]

In some ways, the crisis of Western culture is as
threatening and alienating as the predicament of the
Israelites taken into exile in Babylon. The passage from
"The Rock" we have just quoted is an echo of the psalmist's lament:[4]

> By the waters of Babylon,
>   there we sat down and wept,
>   when we remembered Zion

On the willows there
   We hung up our lyres
For there our captors
   required of us songs,
And our tormentors, mirth, saying,
   "Sing us one of the songs of Zion!"
How shall we sing the LORD's song
   in a foreign land?

The Israelites at least had the advantage of being exiles in a foreign land; we do not. The moment would come when they would return. But we are exiles in our own land; we cannot reverse either time or our tradition. Our alienation is not merely religious; it is also cultural. It has placed us in the same situation as Sartre's when he summed up his judgment of Faulkner's *The Sound and the Fury* by declaring: *"J'aime son art, je ne crois pas à sa métaphysique."*[5] Which amounts to saying that we have severed Western culture from its metaphysical foundations, from its theological roots, from its sacramental significance, although we still like its art and even more its technology (by which we have impressed the whole world from Ghana to China, including India, for whom Western man is synonymous with technological man). The city of Florence still means much to us, even if it has become a drive-in museum. Western culture and its Christian tradition as a whole today resembles a museum, exhibiting this piece or that to attract the post-Christian tourist.

The drive toward radical immanentism is the sign of our time. Neither a new reformation nor any kind of religious revival will suffice to cope with the exigencies imposed by such a context, regardless of the help—if any—offered by the debilitated institutions that have survived the radical monotheism of the West. Theologians have not considered this handicap with sufficient attention: indeed, they have not admitted to any sort of handicap. Nevertheless, a "Christ without culture" is today just as much a chimera as the "Christ of culture," that "fundamental misfortune of Christendom," according to Kierkegaard. For the sickness of the Christian tradition will not be healed simply by withdrawing, so to speak, Christ from culture. Should Christianity (as some early Christians, like Tertullian, claimed that it must) separate itself from our civilization, it will soon become an enclave of anachronism and cultural impotence. Seen in this light, the difficulty in communicating the gospel assumes the proportions of an insuperable obstacle. That Bultmann's theology has attempted to overcome this difficulty is in itself a guarantee of the seriousness of the obstacle.

No matter how syncretistic the religiosity of the Mediterranean world was in the first century, still it offered certain affinities with the vocabulary of the gospel; one must make this statement not only in spite of but precisely because of the fact that the gospel was a scandal to the Jew and foolishness to the Greek. Today it is not a scandal; nor is it foolishness.

Those who have seen *La Dolce Vita* will remember the first scenes of the film, where the huge crucifix hanging from a helicopter hovers incongruously over the utter indifference of the sunbathers on the rooftops. In other words, Christian symbols no longer make any claim upon us as they did even upon those who thought they were scandalous or foolish.

In *The Art of T. S. Eliot,* Helen Gardner reports an incident that eloquently expresses modern man's immunization to the power of the Christian symbols. She writes: "The most remarkable demonstration I have had of this failure in communication in *Ash Wednesday* was at a tea-party, when a colleague said that the repetition at the close of Section III always suggested to him a drunk man coming home late at night and muttering to himself as he stumbled up the stairs. When someone present objected: 'But it is a phrase from the Canon of the Mass,' he replied: 'How am I supposed to know that; it doesn't mean anything to me.' When someone else added: 'But surely you recognize it as coming from the New Testament?', he answered: 'Well, lots of phrases come out of the Bible ultimately.' "[6] Miss Gardner, a literary critic, concludes: "Even for those who accept the Christian Faith some of the phrases in *Ash Wednesday* have less than their full effect, for to feel their force one needs to be accustomed to use them in the same context as the poet."

To be sure, it is not merely a question of different beliefs. Nor is it only a question of the substitution of a scientific, technological world view for a mythological one, although this substitution has had something to do with the transition from radical monotheism to radical immanentism. The malaise lies deeper, in the desuetude of the Christian tradition and the consequent revision of the presuppositions on which our self-understanding and our world view were based.

"The trouble of the modern age," writes T. S. Eliot in *On Poetry and Poets*, "is not [...] the inability to believe certain things about God and man which our forefathers believed."[7] Indeed, some of our assumptions are just as preposterous and superstitious, just as irrational and absurd. But the trouble is "the inability to *feel* towards God and man as they did." In other words, the core of the gospel and the Christian symbols are contemporaneous with a definite historical situation. (The Christian way and the Western man's way are synonymous for many an African nationalist.) On the other hand, the inaccessibility of the gospel and the Christian symbols will not diminish if we simply identify with the historical situation into which they were born. (The Lord's Supper thus becomes magic, or merely a "symbol"—in the wrong sense of the term—depending on whether such an identification is intended or not.) The Christian tradition might just as well be labeled the imaginary and oral museum of Christian antiquities. This is precisely what happens in *Waiting for Godot*: Question—"Do you remember the Gospels?" Answer— "I remember the maps of the Holy Land. Coloured they were. Very pretty ... that's where we'll go for our honeymoon."[8]

If the Christian symbols have thus lost their claim upon man's consciousness and their power to command his mode of being, it is not modern man in his present cultural context who will restore these to them. His inaptitude for the reality of God's transcending presence would prevent him from doing so. Like Weber, who complained about it occasionally, modern man's soul is *"religiös unmusikalisch."*[9] It is not attuned to the divine. Sign of progress? or of retrogression? The same event can present both aspects. "The evolution of mankind toward the rationality of positive science was for Comte a distinctly progressive development," writes Eric Voegelin in *The New Science of Politics;* but "for Weber it was a process of disenchantment *(Entzauberung)* and de-divinization *(Entgöttlichung)* of the world."[10] Recovering from our disenchantment, there is only one thing for us to do—to "recognize that the world has grown godless" (Jaspers).[11]

Now the significant thing is that this disenchantment has two aspects. On the one hand, it has been a disenchantment with religion or the counterfeit of it: Modern skepticism, Walter Stace[12] has pointed out, was not so much caused by the scientific revolution as by a latent readiness to forsake the Christian tradition. On the other hand, there has also been a disenchantment with science (cf. the chapter on Hawthorne). The signs that point to it are perhaps less obvious, but they become real now and then, when the prospects of total annihilation threaten us.

Whether we like it or not, it is not possible to transplant a tropical tree to a northern climate and hope that it will grow—unless nature should change its course. This applies not only to vegetation but also to the Tree of the Cross as well as to all the other symbols of the Christian tradition. And if our culture has grown cold to the symbols of the gospels, what more could one hope for, than that it might change its course?

After all, this has happened before. It was by becoming non-Jewish that the gospel entered the Hellenistic world. Thanks to this foothold in Hellenistic culture, Christianity spread from one Greek city to another, until the promulgation of the Edict of Toleration, which ushered in the Constantinian phase of Western culture, and Christianity gradually became the official religion of the Empire.

What is needed is not so much a theological reformation as a cultural revolution.

Every culture rises from a substratum of religiosity, and grows both reflecting and deflecting the specific characteristics of that particular religiosity. But no culture can ever rise higher than the tower of Babel, regardless of the quality of its religious foundations and accoutrements. What is happening now is that the religiosity of Western culture—its foundations shaken and its accoutrements wearing out—at last is revealed for what it truly is, namely, the paraphernalia of faith in God. Although Christianity is by no means synonymous with, or bound to, the cultural paraphernalia of this religiosity, nevertheless these are typically Western as well as Christian. And, by the same token, they are caducous. Ironically, it is what the Christian tradition has achieved—in a word, Western culture—that has become caducous, especially if it is seen in the light of non-Western religiosities. Christianity is thus known (or misknown) by its culture. But this culture has succeeded in both naturalizing and neutralizing Christianity by finally revealing that its so-called triumph since Constantine was simply a damper put on the ambiguous religiosity that is the lot of every man.

In other words, we have domesticated the universe, or so we think, but we have lost the cipher of its symbols, we have estranged ourselves from it. We have "desacralized" the world, forgetting that ultimately culture is a consecration of the world. Accordingly, a transfiguration of culture is the most urgent task of the present day.

But this is a cultural task; it cannot be the result of any revival. To this task we are all obligated. It is the cultural obligation of post-Christian man, be he a theologian or not, Christian or not. Indeed, Western culture is already groping beyond this devaluation of its symbols for a new dialect, for a new language. *"C'est la même époque,"* writes Paul Ricoeur, *"qui tient en réserve la possibilité de vider le langage, en le formalisant radicalement, et celle de le remplir à nouveau, en se remémorant les significations les plus pleines, les plus lourdes, les plus liées par la présence du sacré à l'homme.*"[13] Or, in the words of the psalmist:

> Whither shall I go from thy Spirit?
> Or whither shall I flee from thy presence?
> If I ascend to heaven, thou art there!
> If I make my bed in Sheol, thou art there![14]

To conclude, the Christian era has bequeathed us the "death of God," but not without teaching us a lesson. God is not necessary; that is to say, he cannot be taken for granted. He cannot be used merely as a hypothesis, whether epistemological, scientific, or existential, unless we should draw the degrading conclusion that "God is reasons." On the other hand, if we can no longer assume that God is, we may once again realize that he *must* be. God is not necessary, but he is inevitable. He is wholly other and wholly present. Faith in him, the conversion of our human reality, both culturally and existentially, is the demand he still makes upon us, the choice he confronts us with. "But when the Son of Man comes, will he find faith on earth?"[15]

II.
Between History and the Eternal

****

My *God*, my *God*, Thou art a *direct God*, may I not say a *literall God*, a *God* that wouldest bee understood *literally*, and according to the *plaine sense* of all that thou saiest? But thou art also (*Lord* I intend it to thy *glory*, and let no *prophane misinterpreter* abuse it to thy *diminution*) thou art a *figurative*, a *metaphoricall God* too: A *God* in whose words there is such a height of *figures*, such *voyages*, such *peregrinations* to fetch remote and precious *metaphors*, such *extentions*, such *spreadings*, such *Curtaines* of *Allegories*, such *third*

Heavens of *Hyperboles,* so *harmonious eloquutions,* so *retired* and so *reserved expressions,* so *commanding perswasions,* so *perswading commandments,* such *sinewes* even in thy *milke,* and such *things* in thy *words,* as all *prophane Authors,* seeme of the seed of the *Serpent,* that *creepes,* thou art the *Dove,* that flies. O, what words but thine, can expresse the inexpressible *texture,* and *composition* of thy *word;* in which, to one man, that *argument* that binds his faith to beleeve that to bee the Word of God, is *the reverent simplicity* of the Word, and to another, the *majesty* of the Word; and in which two men, equally pious, may meet, and one wonder, that all should not understand it, and the other, as much, that any man should.

—John Donne[1]

NATHANIEL HAWTHORNE:
The Obsolescence of God

✳✳✳ ✳✳✳✳✳✳✳✳✳✳✳✳✳✳✳✳✳✳✳✳✳✳✳✳✳

Most of the outstanding works of contemporary literature, like Camus's *The Plague* or *The Stranger*, affirm an atheistic view of man's situation. A rare few, like *Barabbas*, by Pär Lagerkvist, solicit neither theism nor atheism, until, in their agonizingly agnostic ultimacy, they are as exigent as a leap into faith or a refusal of transcendence if accepting transcendence should mean its devaluation. The confrontation between theism and atheism constitutes the theme of yet another category of novels, best exemplified by Dostoevski's *The Brothers Karamazov*.

Hawthorne's particularity lies in the fact that he shows how, to put it briefly, theism slips into atheism. It is the special merit of this author to have drawn our attention to the inevitable degradation of the religio-cultural structures that were meant to incarnate the faith. There can be no faith without an attendant culture; even the purest faith must incarnate itself into forms, institutions, or customs as well as rites, by which it is also betrayed. That event which appears as the greatest hour of faith may the next minute terminate into a superstitious conformism; faith can be crippled by its own purity, as well as by the organs that express it. As a matter of fact, theologians are well aware that those who seek to preserve the purity of faith usually surrender it to the legalistic rigorism of the *regula fidei*.

At once a realist and a good theologian, Hawthorne not only knows that every act of faith presupposes a cultural context in which it necessarily inserts itself and takes root, but also that the purity, the authenticity of faith is least determined, if at all, by the measure in which it excludes itself from the cultural setting. On the other hand, he knows too that the framework of culture is per se neither guaranty nor guardian of the purity of faith. Clothes are no absolute indication of a man's quality. Good shoes are made by a good shoemaker, whether he is a Christian or not. Likewise, cultural patterns, which result from the action of faith, are essentially neutral and when the faith has outgrown them —as it must sooner or later—they tend to petrify or "nationalize" it.

Hawthorne realized both the "dynamics of faith" and

the servitude to which it is bound and upon which it fails. Culture is both the expression of faith and of its degradation: the purity of faith is measured by the extent to which it is embodied in cultural patterns and authenticates them as well as is authenticated by them. But the manna that daily descended upon the Israelites in the wilderness could not be hoarded from one day to the next without being spoiled. The same is true of faith. It cannot be hoarded. No civilization, no society, no church, no creed, can attempt to hoard faith and not degenerate. Such is the background against which many characters of Hawthorne's literary creation manifest their situation.

In Hawthorne's work we are witness to a world that is about to undergo, or is in the process of undergoing, the transition that has most affected the relevance of the Christian tradition to Western culture. Hawthorne shows how, in retrospect, the transcendental conception of the universe has lost its vitality and how the more it becomes crystalized, the more it can paralyze the society in which it fossilizes the faith. When faith thus becomes rigid totalitarian doctrine, religion turns into superstition; and the transcendental vision of man's destiny capitulates before an immanentist conception of the universe.

However, we must also note that Hawthorne is so meticulous in his reconstitution of the Puritan society as to suggest that what now appears to be its servitude was once the occasion for its grandeur. In the world that he depicts, the rupture with the Christian tradition has not yet been consummated; from his vantage point what good things the Puritan experiment has achieved can still be felt, but they are remote enough to bespeak the latent obsolescence of the Christian tradition. Hawthorne thus anticipates the major dilemma of our century by plainly hinting that Christendom itself gave birth to the post-Christian era.

Where he succeeds in particular is in showing that it is not without some hesitation that man dismisses his God. And yet, in spite of the obvious religious framework that supports the Puritan community and its activities, Hawthorne shows that God has already become an anachronism. Faith in God is a living reality that kills and makes alive. But the religion of the community seeks nothing other than to erect itself as a mausoleum for its mummified God. This happens whenever man's natural inclination to believe in something beyond dispute, or whenever logical consistency, whether of the rational or of the superstitious type, overcomes faith and canonizes the personal and social structures of being this faith has brought about. Within a religious framework, such an attitude both engenders and is born of perfectionism; perfectionism is but the religious disguise of man's pretension to become like God, the self-righteous and perverse hallowing of man's attempt to deify himself.

Perfectionism inevitably turns God into a policeman, or a witch-hunter—a Grand Inquisitor. One need not

exaggerate to suggest that many of Dostoevski's characters have their prototypes in those of Hawthorne: Aylmer and Chillingworth adequately prefigure Ivan Karamazov, while Aminadab announces Smerdyakov, and
Dimmesdale's faith is the tragic version of Alyosha's.
Ivan's intellectual pride leads him to the assumption that
there may be no God. Perfectionism, or the Puritan
community's spiritual pride, is but a reluctant disavowal
of God's reality and the Christian tradition has already
become a dead letter.

The deliquescence of this tradition, Hawthorne aptly
observes, does not result from any rationalist or scientific attack upon Christianity. Neither reason, nor science
and technology are in themselves inimical to faith. In
the beginning of "The Birthmark" Hawthorne, citing
electricity and taking note of the recent discoveries of
science, remarks how the love of science can rival the
love of woman.[1] The reader is tempted to think that,
since Aylmer's scientific passion overshadows his love
for his wife, he has already exalted his scientific pursuit
into some sort of religious quest. But as Hawthorne
clearly intimates, Aylmer's problem does not originate
in any conflict between science and religion; it stems
from his investing science with the attributes of religious
perfectionism; which means that just as there can be a
pseudoreligion arrogating to itself the prerogatives of
science, so also there can be a pseudoscience parading
in the vestments of religion.

It is one thing to develop the technical knowledge acquired through the efforts of science; it is another to substitute such knowledge for that existential knowledge which, as religion holds, cannot be measured by any scientific means. That such a temptation is quite human need not be doubted; but this does not prevent its resulting in the debasement of one human being by another, as Hawthorne himself shows in another short story, "Rappaccini's Daughter," in which Beatrice states: "My father's love of science . . . estranged me from all society of my kind."[2] If it diminishes man, science has already usurped the rôle of religion or has simply ceased to be objective, as can be seen today in the spectacle of scientific research determined by political or economic ideologies. To be sure, the converse is also true: religion often represents the usurpation of man's dignity and of the intrinsic worth of his situation in the world.

To revert to "The Birthmark," it is significant that Georgianna has been accustomed to considering the epidermic peculiarity on her cheek as a charm, and so had her husband, too, for a long time. But Aylmer is suddenly convinced that, though perhaps the birthmark is a charm, it certainly cannot pretend to be, on Georgianna's cheek, anything but "the visible mark of an *earthly* imperfection." The italics have been added in order to draw attention to Aylmer's pseudoreligious, perfectionist logic. According to such logic, it is obvious that an "earthly" imperfection is but some form of human sinfulness, and to eradicate it could only fulfill the intention of a pious act.

On the surface, Aylmer can thus afford or claim to be respectful of the religious point of view. But he cheats us as well as himself when he regards the birthmark as an imperfection caused by human sinfulness, and invites us to stamp out sinfulness by eradicating the birthmark. What he refuses to acknowledge, actually, is that the blemish is the sign of human finitude, that the whole man, body and soul, wears nothing but the imprint of his finitude. For man sins because he is finite. Aylmer, on the contrary, would regard man as finite because he is sinful. And by removing this sign of human sinfulness, he would also transcend man's finitude.

This is precisely the attitude that governs the tendency to deify oneself. By rejecting the creation with its finitude and all the signs that point to it, Aylmer avows himself as one who suffers from that passion of self-deification which, Hawthorne seems to contend, is a murderous passion. Not only does it rob man of his humanity; it also justifies crime. It violates the principal meaning of the concept of finitude, according to which finite existence never is self-authenticating: ". . . The stain goes as deep as life itself . . ." Finitude is that limitation of human existence which is not in man but is a sort of boundary between man and man, the self and the world—the experience of the otherness thanks to which man stands revealed to himself. Not so for Aylmer. Already in his dream, the knife he plans to use to perform the operation sinks as deep as Georgianna's heart—Aylmer must kill if he is to remove the birth-mark successfully.

But he persists in his demiurgic conviction that the birthmark is a sign of earthly imperfection: "I am convinced of the perfect practicability of its removal,"[3] and encourages himself by saying: "I shall have corrected what Nature left imperfect in her fairest work."[4] From here on the false pretenses that nurture his perfectionism begin to show where the flaw lies. Manifestly, either the law of nature is identified with the divine law or it is not. If it is, its violation means contravening the law of God (which Aylmer claims he wishes to uphold). If it is not, the problem simply becomes more complex but not to the extent that it will cover up Aylmer's sedition against God and his rejection of human finitude. For although he protests that the conquest of nature will terminate in a deeper and more reverential knowledge of God's handiwork and mysterious creation, the same can also, ironically enough, be the perfidious tool of man's alienation.

Surely it is neither science nor technology that must be held responsible for this alienation: it might not have happened had not the Christian tradition, by some inner failure, already prepared the ground for such a development. Hawthorne endeavors to make this point quite clear. The heart of the matter is very simple to grasp. From Hawthorne's point of view, man's "control over nature" is such that it cannot free man himself from his ultimate dependence upon it; he can, however, be deceived by the tools with which he has sought to achieve such a goal.

The deception began, we learn from Aylmer's case, as soon as Georgianna's imperfection was slyly regarded only as an earthly one, implying thereby that its removal must of necessity reveal not only Georgianna's physical but also her spiritual perfection. Indeed, we can almost hear Aylmer protesting that he is not a "materialist" or an atheist. His library contains authors, Hawthorne tells us, who "perhaps imagined themselves to have acquired from the investigation of Nature a power above Nature and from physics a sway over the Spiritual world."[5] As for Aylmer himself, he "redeemed himself from materialism by his strong and eager aspiration towards the infinite."[6] Or so he leads Georgianna to believe.

Naïve and innocent, Aylmer's wife continues to believe in his "spiritual" aspirations and is caught even more inextricably in the meretricious web of her husband's quest for perfection. She admires him, even worships him more than ever. Victim of his own deception, Aylmer himself does not protest. He says: "Ah, wait for this one success, then worship me if you will. I shall deem myself hardly unworthy of it."[7]

When at last the operation is about to take place, he has completely won his wife's admiring submissiveness. But it becomes equally certain that she is offering herself as a sacrifice to his pretension to deity. When the operation is performed Aylmer of course thinks it is successful: "My peerless bride, it is successful! You are perfect." But at what price? The helpless Georgianna has hardly the time to whisper: "Aylmer, dearest Aylmer, I am dying!" And Hawthorne concludes: "The fatal hand had grappled with the mystery of life, and was the bond by which an angelic spirit kept itself in union with a mortal frame."[8]

One cannot conquer time or violate nature with impunity, while existence entails contingency and being is but the courage to be "in the frail effulgence of eternity." By not realizing that man's being is the being of that which he is not and that man is not autonomous, Aylmer missed the "profounder wisdom." This wisdom would have consisted in his acceptance of the birthmark not as a sign of imperfection but as a symbol of human finitude, which can be transfigured not by self-deification but only if it is assumed and lived as an act of faith.

Beyond the theme of sin and redemption, which is somewhat limiting, it is the drama of man's inescapable destiny—freely assumed—that more especially constitutes the texture of Hawthorne's world. For him, the notion of natural man can only signify nature-transcending man, man in society or better yet, man's inability to find a home in nature, because nature is essentially indifferent to him. Hawthorne does not view the cosmos as a harmonious whole, if by that is meant a self-asserting, self-evident, self-consistent reality. It was this kind of vision that motivated Aylmer's ambition; he sought to achieve it through science until it was made evident to him that science could not remove the existential question about life and death except through death.

In *The Scarlet Letter*, the Puritan community seeks an identical goal and tries to create it by law, until Arthur Dimmesdale's tragedy shows that it does not lie within the possibility of history or of culture, nor within that of religion. Regardless of which usurps the rôle of the other, both science and religion can sacrifice human finitude to quench their thirst for coherence in the universe as they vainly pursue the quest of logical consistency in man's destiny.

The themes of "The Birthmark" are carried and further developed in *The Scarlet Letter*. With this difference, that Aylmer's rôle now devolves both upon the Puritan community and (so to speak) its *alter ego*, Chillingworth, who is at once Aylmer's counterpart and represents the secular version of codified Puritanism. The latter's rigidity is no less expressive of a will to authenticate itself than Aylmer's determination to achieve perfection, or Chillingworth's to vindicate his own, even through destruction. Indeed, both Chillingworth and the community are, like Aylmer, devoured by a drive for perfection—in obvious contrast to Hester and Dimmesdale.

It might help, at this point, to indicate that we diverge radically from those who would judge the latter's adultery simply from the moralistic point of view. The mark

Hester is made to wear on her dress is, like Georgianna's birthmark, but the symbol of human finitude, the violation of which is worse indeed than an infraction of the moral code. Hester knows the difference, which, self-righteously, the community as well as Chillingworth chooses to ignore. Chillingworth asks: " 'But, Hester, the man lives who has wronged us both! Who is he?' 'Ask me not!' replied Hester Prynne firmly, looking firmly into his face. 'That thou shalt never know!' "[9] But he is determined to know, by means of a procedure that will equate Dimmesdale's bodily disease and spiritual ailment, and recall Aylmer's so-called spiritual aspirations. It is Chillingworth who violates, "in cold blood, the sanctity of a human heart," as Dimmesdale says to Hester; "Thou and I, Hester, never did so!"[10] Chillingworth is in this enterprise but the executioner of the Puritan community, in whose midst he has taken up residence.

Of remarkable intelligence, this alchemist-like scientist succeeds in becoming Dimmesdale's parishioner and physician at the same time. He is a parasite, but not to a lesser degree than is the religious perfectionism of the community, which perfectionism he now is going to vindicate while at the same time revenging himself. To be sure, there is a difference between the individual and the community: like Aylmer, Chillingworth has set himself above human finitude, whereas the Puritan community simply forgets that it is not exempt from, or immune to, sinfulness. But this difference is inconsequential. As Hawthorne declares in the conclusion of *The Scarlet Letter*, "in the view of Infinite Purity we are sinners all alike."[11] And though our sinfulness, like Dimmesdale's, only "burns in secret," no innocence can be worn less sinlessly than Hester's red letter "A." Hester, indeed, looks like a madonna, though "only by contrast." For in her case, "there was the taint of deepest sin in the most sacred quality of human life, working such effect, that the world was only the darker for this woman's beauty, and the more lost for the infant she had borne."[12] Like Pearl, for whose birth "a great law had been broken," innocence is both our happiness and our torture. ("She is my happiness! She is my torture!" exclaims Hester, "the likeness of the scarlet letter" with which she adorns her finitude.[13])

Thus, the conflict between sin and redemption is but the apparent theme of *The Scarlet Letter*, according to which Dimmesdale's and Hester's suffering brings to light the bond of solidarity that unites all men under a condition of finitude and sinfulness. The deeper theme of Dimmesdale's and Hester's tragedy deals with the incompatibility between the religious-like, Promethean pretensions of perfectionism and the fundamentally utopian character of faith in God. Whereas the latter is prompted by a man-honoring and world-facing motive, and corroborates a type of attitude centered in the paradoxical conviction that God is "human," the former is set in motion by the presumption that man is divine. The former is iconoclastic and, consequently, *for* man, precisely when it confesses that God is human—which means that God is not what man himself would be if he were God. The latter is idolatrous, because it would re-create man as *man* would like to have created him had *he* been God. It is on an unambiguous recognition of this capital difference between a utopian faith in God and a perfectionistic religiosity that our understanding of *The Scarlet Letter* ultimately hinges.

In this light, Hawthorne's novel raises the question how, within the context of the Puritan experiment, the Christian tradition from iconoclastic became perfectionistic and swerved from its utopian purpose. The answer is, by letting utopianism degenerate into other-worldliness. While the utopian approach to the world may be described as one that is meant to transfigure it in the name of God's transcending presence, otherworldliness implies the denial of this world for the sake of another. Being iconoclastic, utopianism renders to the world what is the world's and to God what is God's, whereas otherworldliness succumbs to its essentially perfection-istic drive and misconstrues the original symbolism of the "other" world into "the other world," and projects it into the future, above and beyond time and space as experienced on this earth. Otherworldliness is therefore often accompanied by legalistic or apocalyptic emphases that predicate almost constantly an attitude of with-drawal from this world on the part of its adherents. In this sense, the Puritan community of *The Scarlet Letter* does belong to another world, a world to which we can hardly "feel the tie." And of which Aylmer and Chillingworth both represent the secular version.

At the same time, as the Puritan community seems to demonstrate, otherworldliness also seeks to safeguard one spot of ground as the true home of religion, as the promise of some heavenly Jerusalem laid in the afterlife. But the notion of the Kingdom of God, in which the utopianism of the Christian tradition is grounded, refers in biblical thought to a mode of being in the world without being of it, of being at home in it as only a pilgrim. For the Kingdom of God is not merely the continuation of this world's kingdoms; neither is it to be built or inaugurated from on high upon the ruins of this world. The Kingdom of God, here and now, begins with the transfiguration of the cultural structures of each specific human reality in every epochal manifestation of its consciousness. Time and eternity, the absolute and the contingent, the sacred and the secular are felt, experienced, in and through the same human event. This implies not a denigration but a valuation of history and of man's involvement in the world: man can freely assume his God-bound destiny and become that which he is not—the new being, *i.e.*, a reintegrated person, who stands revealed to himself even while he hears God's question to Adam, to every man: Where art thou? As Dimmesdale says to Chillingworth: "Were I worthy to walk there [in heavenly Jerusalem], I could be better content to toil here."[14]

Man can hide himself, or he can overreach himself.

He does not want questions, but answers; not to seek the Kingdom of God but to settle down in the commodities of history, the convenient catalogues of religious and cultural customs. But existence is not a custom. Life is not a habit, enshrined in social or ecclesiastical institutions. And when existence becomes a custom, then it pays the price for the compromises on which institutions, moral codes, and systems of belief must necessarily rest, as Dòstoevski's Grand Inquisitor makes plain. And always the price is man's dignity. Existence is ambiguous.

Admittedly, it is because of this ambiguity that man, as Baudelaire has said, is a postulation both toward God and toward Satan. And it is this twofold postulation that permits us to see in Aylmer's spiritual aspirations the disguise of his self-glorification, and in the community's morality the mask of its incapacity for God's grace, for the Kingdom of God. Neither angel nor brute, man compromises: both perfectionism or self-deification, as the case may be, are the insatiable measure of his ambiguities, their idolatrous expression. And idolatry, under which come perfectionism and self-deification, constitutes in the last analysis the ultimate negation of the utopian character of religion, as do, because they too are idolatrous, institutions, conventions, beliefs, or moral codes—all of which sacrifice the inner life, the self, which can be adjusted to, or measured by, no evasion of authentic existence.

But religion often evades existence. It withdraws from

the world. Indeed, it can violate the sanctity of the human heart. Even then, however, religion only reveals that which it seeks to hide, namely, man's finitude; "Not a stitch in that embroidered letter but she has felt it in her heart."[15] There is a direct progression from the sanctimonious, holier-than-thou pretension of the Puritan community to Chillingworth's and Aylmer's quest for logical consistency to the metaphysical rebellion of Dostoevski's Ivan or Kirilov. In each case, the motive is the same. Saint Augustine summed it up admirably in his *Confessions* when he wrote: "Subject to change . . . I should rather suppose that thou art mutable than not being myself what thou art."[16] Which in this context means that in his avidity for perfection, or self-sufficiency, man would rather have an imperfect God—an idol that eventually looked like himself—than not be what God is. In other words, religion can be atheistic, just as atheism can be religious.

In biblical thought, perfection means letting God be God and conversely that man must assume his finite condition. It also means that God is not that principle by which man could explain everything and understand himself as he would explain any mechanism regardless of its complexity. For not only existence itself is a question mark raised against man's understanding of it, but also, more importantly, the question of existence is such that it does not lead to God, though it should. Man is therefore left with no other responsibility than assuming the limitations of the human reality, if he wants to assert its intrinsic worth. But perfectionism seeks to elicit the question of God out of the question of existence by fancying God as the mere continuation of man. Not only, hence, does perfectionism "freeze" God, it also robs man of his nature, it "denatures" him. Also, in the biblical view, man is a sinner, not in himself, but before God: man can stand before God only as a sinner. Perfectionism, by contrast, upsets the dialectic of this relationship between God and man, and would claim for man the possibility of achieving sinlessness, supposedly prior to standing before God. Perfectionism is unaware of the fact that sinlessness would actually make God superfluous: man would be authenticating, or redeeming, himself.

The self-contradiction inherent in such a project is underscored by Hawthorne when he tells us that "infinite purity" is what makes us all sinners alike.[17] We are all finite and incapable of infinitude, except inasmuch as we fail to achieve it. For the letter "A," which apparently means "adulteress" and could also mean "angel," actually stands for "Adam," the creature on whom the letter is "too deeply branded" for him to reveal his "fellow-sinner's and fellow-sufferer's name" and thereby to exonerate himself from the weight of finitude. For the weight of finitude, not the exhibition of world-denying perfectionism, is the true measure of authentic existence.

In the higher Christian tradition, never was the City of God to be realized at the price of the terrestrial city of man: God's design does not destroy man's destiny.

The Kingdom of God is not the estuary of human society, but its constant motivation. Societies come and go and the mantle of their contingent religiosity varies with time and space. They will never result in the Kingdom of God. The complex of human activities, social, political, cultural, or religious, will never approximate such a degree of perfection as to reach ultimately the Kingdom of God. Nor will man be so perfect, so sinless, as to become like God. The failure to acknowledge this was the error of the Puritan community.

The Kingdom of God, which is not a possibility of history, always stands in judgment upon history, upon man's achievements. In other words, the Kingdom of God, or eternity, is the principle of historical self-criticism. The Pilgrim Fathers apparently knew what this entailed. Lest we should overlook this factor in reading *The Scarlet Letter*, Hawthorne draws our attention to it in the very first chapter of his novel. "The founders of a new colony," he writes, "whatever Utopia of human virtue and happiness they might originally project, have invariably recognized it among their earliest practical necessities to allot a portion of the virgin soil as a cemetery and another portion as the site of a prison."[18] The communion of saints is a communion of sinners. The nearer a man comes to God, the more remote he is from him. The same holds true for societies and for religious institutions or beliefs. A confession of faith is at the same time a confession of sins, of doubt, of man's incapacity for faith.

The founders of New England colonies recognized

this when, in their utopian faith, they allotted "a portion of the virgin soil as a cemetery and another portion as the site of a prison." Long before W. H. Auden, they knew that the roots of democracy are more firmly planted when they are in the soil of the confession of sins. This lesson, the Puritan community of *The Scarlet Letter* had forgotten. But by beginning his novel at the site of a prison, Hawthorne reminds us that the fall of man, or human finitude, though it does limit, cannot altogether frustrate man's utopian project toward authentic existence. What falsifies it is rather the perfectionism of religiosity, which, no less than Aylmer or Chillingworth, violates the sanctity of the human heart. Hawthorne's understanding of human nature thus presents some affinity with Dostoevski's, a few of whose novels end, roughly speaking, at the door of a prison or its equivalent.

Hawthorne reveals the gradual dishabilitation by which the Christian tradition will subsequently surrender to the claims of post-Christian man. Unlike "the founders of a new colony," post-Christian man vies with religious perfectionism by agreeing with Ivan Karamazov in postulating his innocence. Atheism, or self-deification, is the form that this postulation of one's innocence has taken in our day. Not insignificantly, in *The Scarlet Letter*, a rosebush has grown on one side of the prison portal.

Flower of Venus, goddess of love, the rose was the symbol of victory, pride, and triumphant love for the ancient Romans. In the Christian tradition, it symbolizes martyrdom or purity, depending on whether it is red or white. As the symbol of the Virgin Mary, it is represented without thorns.[19]

But there is no need to overburden the rather casual parallelism between Mary and Hester Prynne, who looked like the Madonna "but only by contrast." It is Pearl who interests us, and especially her confrontation with the Governor. The incident takes place at his mansion; Governor Wilson is actually checking on how well the child is being brought up in the Christian faith and asks her who made her. Pearl replies "that she had not been made at all, but had been plucked up by her mother off the bush of wild roses that grew by the prison-door."[20] A child's answer to be sure. But a rather telling statement, when one admits that Pearl grew up at a time when the catechism was still the charter of man's destiny, investing daily existence with a sacral intensity. Pearl's reply already contains the seed of the innocence that subsequently Western man will claim for himself in parting with the God of the Christian era.

Hester's and her child's exclusion from the community is motivated, at least externally, by her transgression. Since the offense had taken place and was already expiated when the novel begins, what irks the community is not so much Hester's misconduct as the fact of being frustrated in its spiritual pride because of Hester's silence about the identity of her lover. It is not the sin so much as this reminder of human finitude, namely, the denial of spiritual perfection, that the community refuses to tolerate. And this seems to be the reason *The Scarlet Letter* does not end with Hester's defeat or Dimmesdale's exposure, for "we are all sinners alike," but with the defeat of a self-righteous Christian community that, having lost the sense of its former utopian vision, had settled down in the self-complacent institutions of absolutism.

When even the catechism seems to be useful only because it hallows these institutions and promotes this absolutism, instead of being a sort of preamble to a declaration of faith in the sovereignty of God, then the transition from radical monotheism to radical immanentism will not be long delayed. Man's commitment to God and his involvement in the world are merely a symbolic indication of the reality of God's sovereign presence. No figure of Yahweh is to be found inside of the Ark of the Covenant: it remains empty and signifies that God's majesty dwells among men, but is not placed under their trusteeship. God cannot be held captive as the Puritan community tries to hold him.

It is no wonder then that the drama of *The Scarlet Letter* is not a moral but a spiritual one. The novel unfolds before us the tragedy of a declining Christian culture: "O Father in heaven," exclaims Hester, "—if Thou art still my Father."[21] Blasphemy?— No. How could it be, since the "Temple" has been occupied by money-changers? Since the word "God" has lost its meaning in the language of the community where Hester is ostracized. But the innocent Pearl, in whose developing character emancipation from the Puritan community, and through it from the Christian tradition, is being personified, is without excuse when she declares: "I have no heavenly Father."[22]

Of course she still is only a child when she makes this declaration. But the important thing is that it is made not out of malice but out of her spontaneous innocence. And furthermore her sentence rejoins and reinforces, not without correcting it, the prying Chillingworth's spurious statement, which at this point, and only at this point of our analysis, we can endorse: "A bodily disease, which we look upon as a whole and entire within itself, may after all, be but a symptom of some ailment in the spiritual part."[23] And what an ailment! Nothing less than the obsolescence of the Christian idea of God and Western man's disavowal of the Christian tradition. Indeed, the crisis of *The Scarlet Letter* prefigures many of our contemporary dilemmas and among them the essential one, namely our cultural incapacity for a sclerotic religiosity whose word for God is not translatable into our idiom.

HERMAN MELVILLE:
Fugitive from God

✳✳✳✳✳✳✳✳✳✳✳✳✳✳✳✳✳✳✳✳✳✳✳✳✳✳

THE attraction that *Moby Dick* has for us today may
be due in part to the fact that it is an adventure story,
and there are few, if any, adventure stories among
contemporary novels of universal significance. But it
may also, and more significantly, be due to the fact that
we recognize in Melville's novel many of those same
qualities that characterize the malaise of recent literature—a literature of no-exit situations, about men
struck by some plague or suddenly snatched from their
technological world by some myth, ancient as that of
Sisyphus, or modern, like that of Yoknapatawpha
County.

Melville is an interpreter of man's perennial quest
for being. But not only does he put into relief the

typically Western character of this quest and its debt to the Christian tradition; he puts that tradition itself into question.

What is there in common between Abraham and modern man? What resemblance between Abraham's adventure story and Captain Ahab's? What common ground is there between Abraham's adventure into faith and Ahab's thralldom to unfaith? *Moby Dick* raises these questions.

Not explicitly and not directly, to be sure. One could go so far as to say that Melville even seeks to complicate our questions by intertwining many themes of the biblical tradition, evoking at one and the same time the legend of Abraham and King Ahab's unfaithfulness, the dreams and visions of Nebuchadnezzar and Belshazzar, Job's triumphant grief and Jonah's reluctant mission; and, as if to show that we have stemmed the stream of the biblical tradition or invalidated any possibility of its relevance to our situation, by evoking also the reprobation of Ishmael—Ishmael, the half-brother of Isaac and son of Abraham and Hagar, the father of another human adventure, the Hegira, as well as Melville-Ishmael, the narrator of this composite description of man's quest for being. Trying to harmonize or assimilate such a multiplicity of themes, each of which is indicative of a different aspect of the human reality, a lesser novel would have broken apart and its author would have produced only a parody of man's condition.

Melville's purpose, in commingling so many and

such varied themes, is not to lengthen his story or fatten his characters, but to show that a real man is never exhausted by his name or a good novel by its number of words, that life is not the monopoly of Western culture, that the human reality can be typified neither by the white nor by the black race alone, neither by the Christian nor by the pagan, and—one might add in these days of messianic pretensions—that the destiny of man does not rest either with the proletarian or the capitalist, with the East or the West, exclusively. To this, Melville seems to add an afterthought: Christianity should have taught us all this, but it has lost its priority among the religions of the world, lost it as soon as Western culture lost its hegemony with regard to the pursuit of happiness. This we learn from the important rôle played by Queequeg—who is the real iconoclast, not Ahab. Ahab merely seeks to dethrone God, but Queequeg proves himself a true iconoclast by accepting his finitude, thus refuting Ahab's pretension to deity.

Let us then consider this cannibal, full of tattoos, who yet is capable of civilized overtures. "It is marvelous how essentially polite they are," observes Ishmael-Melville. Some will doubtless see in this observation a trace of romanticism, and perhaps with good reason. However, we cannot help sensing it as the iconoclastic wedge of Melville's implicit critique of the Christian tradition, for he adds, in a humorous but Delphic comparison, that "Queequeg was George Washington cannibalistically developed."[1] "Self-collected" and "without creditors," this "simple honest heart" acts like "a crea-

ture in the transition stage—neither caterpillar nor but-
terfly."

As sophomoric a truth as this may seem, Melville invites us to reflect on it today. On the other hand, from
our Christian culture we have acquired the habit of over-
looking the fact that human existence will remain a
mystery, whether or not one believes in God, or aban-
dons Christianity and bows down to technology; on the
other hand, neither religion nor civilization will ever
prevent us from deluding ourselves. Man is always in a
transition stage, neither angel nor beast, neither good
nor evil. "You cannot hide the soul,"[2] as Melville says
of Queequeg; it is that which keeps us at equal distance
from the angel and from the beast.

Finally, Queequeg's iconoclastic rôle is underlined
by means of some additional information that at first
seems quite incidental. It is because of Queequeg that
Ishmael is at last convinced that "since Christian kindness has proved but hollow courtesy"[3] the Christian way
of life has become a way of hiding the soul. No less
ironic is the fact that Queequeg had originally wanted
to learn from the Christians the art of making his people
even happier than they were, and true to themselves. But
he finds that neither truth nor happiness (or authentic
existence) is determined by geography. He was a prince,
born on an island far away to the West and to the South
—an island, Melville adds in a statement that is equally
valid poetically and philosophically, which "is not down
on any map; true places never are."[4]

Home is nowhere. Nor is the soul any place where it

can be hid, even with the help of a religion whose claim to truth relies more on topography (as Pascal would have said) than on radical obedience to the God who is the creator of all mankind. No more than the Israelites' solemn assemblies and their ritual sacrifices (through which they congratulated themselves), can Christianity claim to occupy the center of man's spiritual geography. In connection with Queequeg, as in the case of Cyrus, the Persian whom Yahweh calls his "messiah," one has, indeed, the impression of hearing again the complaint of the prophets of ancient Israel scoring the idolatrous comfort and spiritual laziness into which their contemporaries' religiosity had sunk.

By reading *Moby Dick* against the biblical background, not only do we not violate the integrity of the novel, we discover certain elements that prove themselves indispensable to a better understanding of the story. For example, Melville's character Elijah may seem to play an ephemeral rôle, but the significance of Elijah is that he helps us to grasp the existential theme of the narrative. At the outset he upsets the applecart, just as the Prophet Elijah (whose name signifies "Yahweh is my God") was the troubler of Israel, when Captain Ahab's namesake was king. Both the king and the captain are usurpers: the king, by abandoning the cult of Yahweh for the Baal cult of his wife, Jezebel, as well as by grabbing Naboth's vineyard—an action for which the prophet denounces him; the captain (who likewise is ominously warned by Elijah), by sailing out of Nantucket on Christmas Day, that is to say, by his willful inobservance of this holy day on which is celebrated the birth of the Word become flesh, and, as it were, by substituting his word for the Word of God. Nothing will now stop Ahab in his visions of self-aggrandizement. The ensuing drama, which is thus motivated by one man's hubris—Ahab's determination to deify himself —also stresses the strict connection between idolatry and self-deification and brings to light their fundamentally usurpative character: both conceal a similar appropriation of oneself and display a mode of being through which existence leaks and, like a ship, founders and sinks.

Self-deification is an inclination that we follow as naturally as we conceive of God in our image, for behind every worshiper lurks a Narcissus. Unable always to distinguish between appearance and reality, man idolizes himself and turns life into an "ungraspable phantom." But let us read Melville himself: "Why upon your first voyage as a passenger, did you yourself feel such a mystical vibration, when first told that you and your ship were out of sight of land? Why did the Persians hold the sea holy? Why did the Greeks give it a separate deity, and own brother of Jove? Surely all this is not without meaning. And still deeper the meaning of that story of Narcissus, who because he could not grasp the tormenting, mild image he saw in the fountain, plunged into it and was drowned. But that same image, we ourselves see in all rivers and oceans. It is the image of the ungraspable phantom of life; and this is the key to it all."[5] Self-apotheosis is, indeed, a mystique, a form of mysticism in which man considers himself the meaning-giving center of the universe—thanks to an optical illusion. Once at sea, for example, it is as if one could never reach the rim of the circle of which one occupies the center. But the circle is without circumference, an appearance without reality. Suffering from a similar illusion, self-deification is in the last analysis like being thrown into the middle of things that have no reality other than their appearance.

But appearance is only what seems to break the kinship between things and beings; it distinguishes them without separating them; it points to and stresses that otherness by which things and beings are what they are. Ultimately, appearance is what preserves the integrity of the intrinsic reality of every thing and being, of the world, and prevents the self from usurping that reality even while being related to it. The sea is the symbol of that ungraspable aspect of reality and, like appearance, it expresses the ultimate impossibility of totally alienating the self by usurping the inalienable reality of things and beings—by usurping oneself. The sea besets us before and behind, all around, like a god. And like a god it reflects one's own image. That is to say, it reflects one's image as only something wholly other than oneself can reflect it. What, then, Captain Ahab rejects is precisely this appearance or rather this otherness by virtue of which man is distinguished from other things and beings, as well as from the Wholly Other, while at the same time, perceiving the reality of his majestic frailty. And, thus alienating himself, Ahab betrays his own reality: he wrecks it.

The relation between the self and the world signifies, when it is properly understood, that man can transcend the world only insofar as he depends on it. Ahab does not grasp this, nor does he realize that man's independence of the world is but the corollary of his dependence on it, and that man's mastery over nature only stresses the irreducible otherness that causes man and nature to be what they are in their interdependence. In his megalomania Ahab imagines, furthermore, that transcendence can result simply from a technical victory over the world, over nature, over Moby Dick—as well as over his own reality.

Ahab has, in other terms, reduced existence to *Dasein*, that is, to the dimensions of a difficult but not impossible technical problem, like the skillful pursuit of a whale. He neglects the fact that existence may be as "ungraspable"—we could even say, "as technically unknowable"—after the most successful whaling trip as it was before, and that man is "other" than all the objective information gathered about him on an IBM card. The conquest of nature is not necessarily a sign of self-transcendence, still less when such a conquest means, as it does for Ahab, the domestication of nature, of the irreducible otherness between things and beings, between man and the world, between man and God, the

Wholly Other. He who seeks to domesticate nature has been enslaved to it; Moby Dick is not, nor ever can be, domesticated. Nor can Ahab, enslaved as he is by this "sickness unto death," domesticate death, become "like gods," and rest in the consummation of his self-deification.

Had Ahab gone into the Whalemen's Chapel, he might have read the inscriptions honoring the memory of those dead in the fulfillment of their human vocation. For there is death in the business of existing: "Yes there is death in this business of whaling—a speechlessly quick chaotic bundling of man into Eternity. But what then? Methinks we have hugely mistaken this matter of Life and Death."[6] Like Ahab, we often mistake this matter of appearance and reality, of self-transcendence and man's dependence on the world; and, reducing existence to the sum total of its objective manifestations, we lower it to a fact among other facts. On the contrary, "take my body who will, take it [Father Mapple declares in stronger terms than we would], it is not me"[7]; rather than a fact, existence is an invocation of hope rooted in "faith [which] like a jackal, feeds among the tombs, and even from these dead doubts . . . gathers her most vital hope."[8] In this respect, Father Mapple's sermon represents the opposite point of view to that of Captain Ahab.

It is relevant to note that Father Mapple is a former sailor and harpooner and that the Chapel, in which he delivers his sermon on Jonah, has a ship's atmosphere, not to mention the seascape on the wall representing a ship tossed by a storm and the sun breaking through the clouds. Like any sailor, Father Mapple knows that the sea is a mirror of existence. But there is such a limpidity of being, such a serenity in his manner of life one would think that the task of existing is different for him than for Ahab; Father Mapple knows and has experienced that "the world's a ship on its passage out, and not a voyage complete; and the pulpit is its prow."[9] The facts of life are basically the same for all—birth and death, the joys and the sorrows; but whereas one will steer a ship as would a castaway, out of defiance, another will do so out of humility, with the sense of vocation, which is symbolized by the pulpit as the prow of a ship (i.e., led by the Word of God in the light of which self-deification ultimately appears as man's "useless passion").

Here, we begin to sense how the topic of Father Mapple's sermon applies to Captain Ahab's inauthentic rebelliousness. Jonah sought to flee worldwide from God to Tarshish, to a land where God would not reign. "But God is everywhere; Tarshish he never reached."[10] Both Jonah and Ahab are fugitives from God. Unwilling to accept existence as a mandate or a pilgrimage, as a mission, life becomes for them a flight. They want, if not to dethrone God, at least to usurp his reign—Ahab through blasphemy and hubris, Jonah through cowardice; the former by trying to wrest his independence vis-à-vis nature, the latter by surrendering to it, so that in the end both abdicate existence.

In contrast to them, Father Mapple points out in his sermon that, as the antithesis of self-deification, self-transcendence implies of necessity the idea of man's dependence on the world. "Mortal or immortal, here I die. I have striven to be Thine, more than to be this world's, or mine own. Yet this is nothing; I leave eternity to Thee; for what is man that he should live out the lifetime of his God?"[11] Or, "I will have no man in my boat, who is not afraid of a whale," as Starbuck puts it, who would rather catch whales and leave eternity to God (perhaps because he would not know what to do with it) and who definitely seems to consider rashness, or self-glorification, a far greater danger than cowardice. And Starbuck probably is right, at least by Aristotelian standards, in distinguishing courage from rashness when it is a matter of whaling. But that is not the whole problem, and Starbuck altogether misses the point by looking the other way, to the ancillary problem of whaling. Indeed, if we faced the real issues (and it is Ahab's behavior that gives us the clue to it), we would realize that more important than the question of whaling is the question of existing. And from this angle, Ahab's behavior no doubt compels us to regard his furious chase after the whale as nothing other than, like Jonah's cowardice, an attempt to evade the responsibility of a dependent existence, the only freedom that can be his.

Just as the business of a whaling ship is to catch whales, so it is the business of a human being to be. But there are as many whales as there are ways of catching them, and Moby Dick is a different whale to the different crewmen. Apart from ostensibly being the monster of Ahab's hatred it is as if in reality Moby Dick put a different question to different people. In particular he is the kind of question mark which Ahab will not or cannot face. Moby Dick thus limits Ahab's hubris as much as he arouses it: there is no escape from finitude, except that which leads to a dead end. This amounts to saying that the reality of the objective world is such that it limits us to ourselves while at the same time inviting us to look beyond ourselves; it questions us, puts us into question, and, at the same time, affirms us. This given and necessary relationship between the self and the world, on the one hand, both confines us and sets us free and, on the other, never obliterates the inscrutability that prevents either element from sublimating the other. Moby Dick's inscrutable malice is Ahab's.

But quite aside from this matter of malice, which is incidental and contingent, what actually is inscrutable is the mystery of Moby Dick's "whaleness" or the mystery of Ahab's being. Hawthorne referred to this inscrutability in a different way. He called it "the sanctity of a human heart," that is to say, the inviolability of every thing and being, of the self, of every "Thou." Blake and Auden after him have said: "Every thing that lives is holy." It does not matter what expression is used, for in the reality that all of these phrases try to grasp it is a question of the mystery of being, of the fact that existence is a mystery and not a problem.

It soon becomes evident, however, that Captain Ahab approaches Moby Dick's and, by the same token, his own inscrutability as a logistic problem. He is interested not so much in whaling as in pursuing a vendetta, the vendetta of a desperately defiant man. But as Kierkegaard has shown in *Sickness Unto Death*, the despair of defiance stems from the weakness of one's will to accept oneself. It is the despair of the suicide or of the blasphemer, the despair of the idolater, the man whose faith is a torment to him, whose existence is a reluctant or rash business, a spiritual suicide. Ahab is the image of that man, though doubtless he is likable, too, as are all men who are vulnerable. "He ain't sick; but . . . he isn't well either. . . . He is a queer man . . . but a good one . . . not a pious good man like Bildad, but a swearing good man—something like me," Peleg says, adding, "only there's a good deal more of him."[12]

His arrogance and evil madness notwithstanding, Ahab wins our affection, and becomes even more likable if we consider him from the standpoint of an average man's ambiguous goodness. After an altercation with Ahab, Stubb has a dream in which he considers it an honor to be kicked by him; our affection still goes to the audacious adventurer even after comparing him with the English captain who lost one arm to Moby Dick and does not want to lose the other. All the same, Ahab is vulnerable, and he knows it when he brags the most— unlike that owner of the "Pequod" who is a "Quaker with a vengeance," and whose description we should find amusing and innocuous, were it not for the fact that it unmasks certain forms of so-called Christian behavior, especially if we remember that beside this Quaker with a vengeance, Starbuck cuts a figure of the Quaker by descent.

Just as it is impossible to be a Christian with a vengeance or a Christian by descent, so also it is impossible for man to be authentic with a vengeance or by descent. The situation on the high seas, which equalizes Christians and pagans, the rash and the cowardly, gradually confronts us with this truth, while prohibiting any escape from it. Bounded as well as unbounded by the sea, man experiences his vulnerability, that is, that existence incurs the threat of nonbeing, incessantly. Defying it will be of no help, and vengeance is a loss of courage in accepting oneself, because authentic existence can only be a matter of faith, of vocation. By lacking faith, Ahab lacks himself, while Starbuck fails his vocation; after all, despite his many condemnations of Ahab's conduct of the ship, Starbuck does not live up to them, being only a Quaker by descent. He forfeits his authenticity. "Even Christians could be both miserable and wicked,"[13] says Queequeg as he draws the inevitable conclusion: "It's a mutual, joint-stock world, in all meridians. We cannibals must help these Christians."[14] Not that Queequeg wishes to deny the supremacy of the Christian religion, which does not seem to affect him one way or the other, nor that Melville is slyly registering the dissolution of Christianity and its hegemony. The important thing is that faith in God is not concerned with what makes us Christians or pagans, because existence is ultimately "but a draught—nay, but the draught of a draught."

With or without God, existence is not a perfectible system; it is as unfinished as the cetological arrangement with which Melville ostensibly distracts us. Not without irony, it is through a fanciful classification of whales that he offers us some essential insights into his conception of human existence.

Like existence itself, he says, cetology is an uncertain science, not merely because it is not systematic enough, but because "in some quarters it still remains a moot point whether a whale be a fish." There is nothing in the classification that Melville proposes that might arouse one's feeling that Moby Dick stands for the evil to be destroyed. Ahab's need for vengeance even becomes the inexplicable expression of a pusillanimous nature. The more one delves into the complexities of cetological classification, the more one is tempted to draw the comparative lessons regarding human existence: it is a moot point whether a man be this or that; depending on the norm, he may be classified in this or that category; and all the statistical data he can gather about himself will not suffice to help him understand himself. What we find most significant in all this is, moreover, that Melville's remarks about man's condition are precisely in agreement with those made by the Christian tradition. The image of God in which man is created signifies nothing other than what Melville hinted at, namely, man's very being remains a mystery to himself, and he can never fulfill it as one can complete the solution of a problem. Therein lies the reason why existence is a draught—the final draught of a draught.

Inasmuch as these reflections on the human reality have been determined by Melville's cetological lucubrations we must add a further remark: Moby Dick does not fit into any classification. He *is*, although he actually is only insofar as he is of a class by itself, much in the same way as this can be said of every man's individual attempt at existence. Unique and yet like other whales, his whiteness itself signifies innocence and evil, purity and death. Why should he be the object of Ahab's hatred? Or why should human existence be both simpler and more complex than Ahab imagined?

In the light of the unfinished cetological classification, the answer is that existence is both simple and complex, because it has no self-evident structure. In itself, it is neither autonomous nor heteronomous. As a task, its execution accomplishes either an act of faith or an act of unfaith, depending on whether one accepts the risk of one's finitude or (like Ahab) defies them by deifying oneself. "Great God! but for one single instant show thyself," cries Starbuck; "never, never wilt thou capture him, old man—In Jesus' name no more of this, that's worse than devil's madness. Two days chased; twice stove to splinters; thy very leg once more smashed from under thee; thy evil shadow gone—all good angels mobbing thee with warnings:—what more wouldst thou have?—Shall we keep chasing this murderous fish till he swamps the last man? Shall we be dragged by him to the bottom of the sea? Shall we be towed by him to the infernal world? Oh, oh—Impiety and blasphemy to hunt him more!"[15] What Starbuck (who also shuns his responsibility and is ultimately as reprehensible as his master) seems to forget, however, is that the line of demarcation between blasphemy and the unconditional act of faith is a tenuous one. And the less he realizes this the more he falters, and the more we begin to dread and take alarm at Ahab's dream of self-deification: relentlessly pursued, it finally achieves its culmination in the chapter of the Doubloon, when, dark and solitary, in the night of his insatiable craving, Ahab himself conducts the litany of his own deification.

Reciting a trinitarian praise to none other than himself, he proclaims, not the birth of some new Adam, but the advent, at last, of man. Unlike Ivan Karamazov, it is not the creation that Ahab rejects, but God himself. Nothing short of his own transfiguration would therefore fully express this rejection. And when the parodic transfiguration quite ceremoniously takes place, Ahab himself appears as both the sacrifice and the sacrificer: "There's something ever egotistical in mountain-tops and towers, and all other grand and lofty things; look here, —three peaks as proud as Lucifer. The firm tower that is Ahab; the volcano that is Ahab; the courageous, the undaunted, the victorious fowl, that, too, is Ahab,"[16] The incantation continues until, in a defiant mood, Ahab accepts the challenge that his own self-deification presents to him, and sanctifies it in words that would recall the passion of the Christ even to the point where Ahab is not so sure of his own divinity: "From storm to storm! So be it, then. Born in throes, it is fit that man should live in pains and die in pangs! So be it, then! Here's stout stuff for woe to work on! So be it, then."[17]

But across the sea, boundless yet bounding us, the words of Father Mapple's sermon ring again in our ears: "Woe to him who would not be true, even though to be false were salvation! Yea, woe to him who, as the great Pilot Paul has it, while preaching to others is himself a castaway!"[18] These words must be underlined, for they explain why Ahab is so likable and so dangerous at the same time. Human, all too human, Ahab is authentically inauthentic, if the phrase is permissible, by contrast with Starbuck's inauthentic authenticity. At least Ahab is bold in his sinfulness, and he sins boldly. But Starbuck, who knows his religion better than Ahab knows his own, who is a better theologian and perhaps a better whaler than Ahab, is capable of no action other than resigning himself to the arrogance and apotheosis of Ahab, the man who after all seeks some manner of salvation, regardless of the cost, even in the desperate path of falsehood.

"The old man seems to read Belshazzar's awful writing," observes Starbuck, who, having himself never inspected the gold coin that Ahab had had nailed to the mast of the "Pequod," now goes to look at the coin. He sees on it "a dark valley between three mighty, heaven-abiding peaks, that almost seem the Trinity, in some faint earthly symbol. So in this vale of Death, God girds us round; and over all our gloom, the sun of Righteousness still shines as a beacon and a hope. If we bend down our eyes, the dark vale shows her mouldy soil; but if we lift them, the bright sun is no fixture; and if at midnight, we would fain snatch some sweet solace from him, we gaze for him in vain! This coin speaks wisely, mildly, truly, but still sadly to me. I will quit it, lest Truth shake me falsely."[19] Daniel, reading the handwriting on the wall, recoiled from proclaiming its awful truth. Starbuck keeps it for himself and almost even from himself, unwilling as he is to proclaim, in Father Mapple's words, "the Truth to the face of falsehood."

The longer the chase lasts, the more diabolic it becomes. The process of self-deification continues as Ahab institutes the sacramental rites by which to celebrate it. It is scarcely possible to miss the usurpative and antidivine intention characterizing the formulary of these rites, which only seem to corroborate Ahab's own usurpation of God's trinitarian attributes. Reversing the traditional Christian formula, as he begins to consecrate the harpoon destined for the White Whale, saying: "Ego non baptizo . . . ," Ahab stands before us not so much the anti-God or God *manqué* as the proud and defiant man, self-reliant and self-sufficient, a man who will not kneel, indeed, who cannot kneel, because he has an ivory leg. Defiance, or pride, rests on an ivory leg, and self-deification thus presupposes but a fatal and desperate repudiation of one's finitude.

Undoubtedly, other interpretations of Ahab's ivory leg have been given, and they may be equally plausible. As for us, adhering to the text as closely as possible, we must point out that Starbuck himself invites us to liken Ahab to Belshazzar, the Babylonian king who saw the fateful handwriting during a banquet, and had succeeded to the throne of his father, Nebuchadnezzar; it was under the latter's reign that Daniel had achieved prominence by being the only one who could explain the king's disturbing vision of a tall statue. This statue was made with different metals from the head, which was of pure gold, to the legs, which were of iron, whereas its feet were a mixture of iron and clay. The fact that in Moby Dick Melville has simply conflated the respective stories of the two kings compels us even more ineluctably to notice that the great Ahab, too, is doomed to fail; his apotheosis, like the dominions of man symbolized by Nebuchadnezzar's statue, is supported by feet of clay, the same clay that also symbolizes the reality of man's finitude.

Regardless of the heights reached, man is ultimately bound to the earth and to his finitude. Human nature is such that it cannot be overcome, not by becoming like God, or by fleeing from God. Jonah never reached Tarshish, where he would be his own master. Self-deification, which is Captain Ahab's Tarshish and the "false" way of transcending one's finitude, always rests on clay pretensions. As Karl Jaspers[20] has remarked, in the process of becoming, man attempts to transcend his finitude but, bound as he is to it, he is finally ruined; existence is destined for shipwreck.

But is this the conclusion that we must finally draw —that existence is bound to be shipwrecked and that man must simply resign himself to such a destiny? Melville himself seems to suggest a negative answer. Some Queequeg is always our bosom friend, often closer to us and truly more like what we are than we ourselves ever can be: "There, then, he sat, the sign and symbol of a man without faith, hopelessly holding up hope in the midst of despair."[21] From stones, God can raise sons to Abraham, should his posterity come to vanish.

Perhaps, the tragedy of Christianity is that it justifies our faithlessness—but precisely that faithlessness is what contradicts human nature, which coerces us always to hope against hope, and ultimately undermines and defeats the most successful attempt at self-deification.

WILLIAM FAULKNER:
Rendez-vous with Existence

****

No WESTERN man today can know where he stands
if he has not gone through Yoknapatawpha County at
least once. As lost as Paradise, this domain is all that
remains for us of the promised land we had been accustomed to or, rather, had been brought up to antici-
pate as the goal of Western culture. Indeed, Faulkner's
world is a historical map of the Christian tradition and
its concomitant culture between twilight and dawn—the
twilight of the Christian era and the dawn of a post-
Christian age. And Yoknapatawpha County is also a
spiritual geography of Christendom, that of a land that
lies more desolate with each generation of lost men, of
renegade Westerners. The geography of a long apostasy,
it cannot be explored except in the light of a central

affirmation, that of a faith that shall prevail, that the world cannot conquer, nor Yoknapatawpha County defeat.

Slow as our awakening has been, we have all by now discovered that we do not need to leave our place in the sun to realize that we do in fact live in Yoknapatawpha County. It is not on any map, simply because, as Melville says, real places are not to be found there. A strange country, the chances are that each discovery will make it even stranger. A country without citizens, citizens without a country: our daily world lies within the limits of Yoknapatawpha County, which are the limits of Christendom, and we are like strangers within our own country. Where else could one be a stranger, except in one's own country? Except in a relationship of mutual strangeness?

Beyond the initial discovery of this mutual strangeness, Camus would have said, everything else is *ipso facto* a construction. A theoretical construction that may, perhaps, describe our situation adequately, but cannot teach us anything about existence; and should it even weigh upon our self-understanding, still such a construction would lack objective certitude.

Everything in Yoknapatawpha County is pervaded with, and conditioned by, that initial strangeness. Every character stands before us as strange as a neighbor—a stranger whether we neglect or imitate him. Either way, all that we can experience is an all-encompassing feeling of estrangement, bound as we are to a situation that in the last analysis merely reflects the present stalemate between Christianity and Western culture. There is no redemptive issue to such a situation, unless a cultural revolution were to stop the decay of Yoknapatawpha County and its spiritual decolonization take place at the same time.

Faulkner's art is characterized by something other than mere technique. The four chapters of *The Sound and the Fury* are four moments of existence: innocence, or prelapsarian sinlessness; the forbidden fruit, or the fall; paradise lost; and redemption. These are rendered without thought for ordinary logical or chronological continuity. Existence is not reducible to a chronological development; making it conform to such a continuity would distort and give a false idea of what in man can never become a measurable quantity.

Faulkner guards against this distortion. Just as behind their apparent regionalism, his novels deploy a universal significance, so is time in Yoknapatawpha County not indicated by chronology, but—whether directly or indirectly—by the fullness of time, the presence of eternity. If Faulkner had, indeed, satisfied himself with one of those traditional devices that would have permitted him to weave the sequences of *The Sound and the Fury* in a chronological development, he would have been merely a *christian* novelist—neither really a novelist nor a Christian. As it is, he proves himself a great novelist—and a theologian, too, without seeming so and without the antiquated apparatus of a forgotten language.

It is not the style of the book that is complex, it is the

Compsons; just as it is not the presence of eternity that is elusive, but time in its chronological infrangibility. Nor is it redemption that is a pipe dream, a crutch, and a pie-in-the-sky, but rather the sound and the fury of existence. It is existence, not destiny, that is missing at the roll call. (Doubtless existence often is like missing an appointment with destiny.)

The absence of chronological sequence serves to corroborate this kind of frustration, just as fate, though under an opposite aspect, strangely plays the same rôle, at least in relation to genealogy if not in relation to chronology. For example, Maury fates Benjy, albeit unsuccessfully since Benjy's name was altered in order not to offend the manes of Maury his namesake. Likewise, Quentin fates his niece Quentin: "I knew the minute they named her Quentin this would happen, Mrs. Compson said. . . . It's in the blood. Like uncle, like niece. Or mother."[1]

The more fatefulness seems to yoke the Compsons to one another, the more purposeless their lives become. Freedom is, in the last analysis, incompatible with purposelessness or with chance, as well as with fate. But neither can there be any freedom without destiny. If destiny is the path of freedom, freedom is the wings of destiny. It is obvious that everything hangs together: fate and emptiness, freedom and destiny, chronology as meaningless mechanical time and time as the presence of eternity, the fullness of time, regardless of any meridian, of the Compsons and the others alike. The absence of chronology allows a greater insistence upon the meaning of man's destiny, just as definitely as Faulkner's outrageous regionalism is the expression of another region, that of the human heart, whatever its longitude and its latitude.

Faulkner's technique is thus the handmaid of his vocation. This supereminent quality he does not share with any other novelist, even though one can detect similarities between him and others. For example, the chronological flashback is a cinematographic invention that others have used. But with Faulkner it acquires another intensity, which we shall discuss presently, just as on a different level, it presents affinities with Joyce's fragmented language. For the time being, let us state that the significant thing is that Faulkner's technique is like the mask of the Japanese noh actor; smaller than the actor's face, the mask is meant not to conceal but to reveal states of the soul. Faulkner's chronological and linguistic flashbacks are the mask through which man stands revealed in the complex of his simplicity. Reality eludes him, but *only the real* can elude him.

What is reality? It is something the structure of which is not self-evident. Beyond the original and unique confrontation between the self and the world, nothing can be said that has any validity. Places are a construction of the mind, and so are the past and the future.

Here and now, that is the only reality. Reality is the fullness of time, the present—but an evanescent present that is related to the chronological constructions of past, present, and future in the same way as my real self is related to the faces I put on. Add or subtract these faces, my real self is something other than their succession. And the novel of a torn conscience, of a fragmented human reality is also something other than what a mere conventional, chronological narration can evoke. If indeed, like a North African river, the narrative appears and disappears it is not simply because the human condition is grasped as a subjective reality only, but because the geographic and objective coordinates of this reality must respond to the notion that one can be a stranger in one's own country. Similarly, if the conventional, chronological structure of time has lost all meaning, Faulkner does not intend to show how man is fettered, weighed upon, fated, by his own past, but rather how, despite everything, the future still remains the virgin soil of constantly new possibilities, of fresh choices, of indefatigable acts of freedom. It is therefore improper to claim that Faulkner suggests man *"vit à reculons,"* that existence is like moving backward.

Consequently, to declare, as André Malraux does in his preface to *Sanctuaire*,[2] that *"l'homme n'existe qu' écrasé"* is only partially true. Otherwise, this would amount to the total elimination of contingency for the sake of a thoroughgoing fatalism on the one hand, and, on the other, of freedom and hope, of the future. For hope depends on contingency as well as on the sense of destiny; this is exactly what the intermittent narrative, the chronological or, even, teleological suspension of time, in the last analysis, bring into evidence.

This effect of Faulkner's style is, I think, indisputable. His is not a universe of despair. On the contrary, hope springs forth constantly, even if at times the heartbeats of the human reality are not sufficient to sustain it. Hope is affirmed even against hope—which is, for us human beings, the way it usually is—despite such passages as: "Of course," Father said. "Bad health is the primary reason for all life. Created by disease, within putrefaction, into decay . . ."[3] Hope is like a clearing through time, as Gabriel Marcel contends in *Homo Viator*,[4] while despair is a sort of consciousness of being walled in by time, *i.e.*, chronological time. For this reason, Marcel adds, hope evinces a prophetic character, not so much by predicting what will happen as by accepting the present and apprehending it as a possibility of the future. We may extend these lines of thought by remarking that, if despair is chronological existence, hope means eschatological existense, that is, an existence that is lived not as a *datum* but as a *mandatum*.

A quick description of some members of the Compson family will reinforce this contention. Let us begin with Caddy. She "doesn't want to be saved" and besides she "hasn't anything anymore worth being saved" for she has "nothing worth being lost that she can lose."[5] She was already two months pregnant when, in 1910, she married a young man from Indiana she had met the summer before at French Lick. Divorced in 1911, she is married again in 1920 to a minor Hollywood magnate. By mutual agreement, they obtain a Mexican divorce five years later. In 1940, Paris is under German occupation. There she vanishes. She reappears at last back home in 1943. About her, Faulkner writes: "Doomed and knew it, accepted the doom without seeking it or fleeing it."[6] She has a daughter, Quentin, whom she has abandoned in care of Jason (who uses her to blackmail Caddy), and who finally climbs down the rain pipe and runs away on the eve of Easter, not without having stolen Jason's money. But it is the date of Easter that is the important thing, as we shall see later on.

Even Jason is not as hopelessly bad as the reader would be inclined to think. A selfish blackmailer, he hates Jews and foreigners, he is cruel to the point of burning circus tickets rather than giving them to the young Luster: "thinking nothing whatever of God one way or the other and simply considering the police"[7] or, which amounts to the same thing morally, simply considering the stock market. He has substituted determinism and probabilism for freedom and destiny, traffic regulation and ticker tape for moral obligation. Faulkner's own judgment is a masterpiece of compactness, filled with irony and harshness, as caustic as it is ambiguous; he presents Jason as "the first sane Compson since Culloden and (a childless bachelor) hence the last."[8] Such is the man who "never had time to be," much like the brother of the prodigal son in the parable told by Jesus. "I never had time to go to Harvard like Quentin or drink myself into the ground like Father. . . ."[9]

One way or the other, the Compson family is doomed.

"The clock tick-tocked, solemn and profound. It might have been the dry pulse of the decaying house itself."[10] But the doom is both apocalypse and revelation, an instrumental description of the hopelessness of time and of hope clearing through time. It is a vindication, namely, that all things are made new again, and a new heaven and a new earth are dawning. To grasp this clearly, we must focus on Benjy and Dilsey.

Benjy, the gelded idiot who is finally sent to the state asylum in 1933, is, together with Dilsey, one of the rare creations of Faulkner's talent, for which he remains unequaled by any other novelist. Time, which is constantly running out on all the other characters, does not affect Benjy. Nor has he substituted a policeman for God, or prefabricated life for authentic existence. Whether structured or divested of all structure, chronological time cannot affect him. What time is it when, having witnessed many deaths, you see a corpse on a movie screen and you smell the odor of death? Benjy smells things. Reliving the past, he smells the presence of past events and people. To him, Caddy smells like apple trees. And through him the absence of chronology shows its real purpose, by indicating that no illusory self-authentication can ultimately destroy the reality of our dependent being and no escape is possible from the ground of being, just as the present cannot be robbed of its concrete actuality in which time is transfigured, redeemed, because the fullness of time is a possibility here and now.

It has been suggested that Benjy is a Christ-figure.

Even if we must at the same time underline the irony of such a parallel in a post-Christian age, the suggestion may be worth considering. What is it based on? As Christ was sacrificed for the sake of Barabbas, so is Benjy sacrificed for the sake of Quentin: "We have sold Benjy's *He lay on the ground under the window, bellowing. We have sold Benjy's pasture so that Quentin may go to Harvard* a brother to you Your little brother."[11] Like Christ, he is thirty-three years old. He typifies innocence because, like Christ again, he is not affected by time, unlike others who run against time or whose time is measured: thus, Quentin's suicide has already taken place while the story of what is leading to it is being told; Jason's chase to recover his money is frustrated by time. By contrast, neither the day nor the hour, if it means withdrawing oneself from full commitment to the present, has any way of altering Benjy's destiny.

It would be possible, of course, to extend the parallelism between Benjy and Christ still further, but sooner or later we must come to this point: since Dostoevski, but doubtless in spite of him, one critic or another has been all too prone to identify with Christ every allegorical idiot in literature. As if being an idiot were all it took to be a Christ-figure! But if one can so easily extend the attributes of Christ, then, indeed, the Christ-event has become meaningless and Christianity has really run out of breath. Unless, of course, those who choose to see in Benjy a Christ-figure also concede that what they mean is a sublimated or subconscious nostalgia for the Christian era. It seems to us that such an interpretation of Benjy is as sterile as it is seemingly original, and does not so much emanate from the integrity of the work itself as from the theological malformation of certain critics. What these critics need are not grandiloquent occasions for Christ-figures, but some simpler kind of truth, something not so farfetched but closer to the dimension of man, and perhaps not so unlike what Dilsey has in mind: "Huh," Dilsey said, "What dey needs is a man kin put de fear of God into dese here triflin young niggers."[12] Nor is the possibility excluded, by the way, that those who, like Dilsey, still believe in God are capable of common sense. In fact, one must turn to Dilsey for a richer understanding of *The Sound and the Fury.*

Undoubtedly, Dilsey is a bridge. She is a bridge between Yoknapatawpha County and the rest of the world; between the Compsons and the rest of mankind, their mediator, so to speak. And she is also a bridge between the Christian past and the present post-Christian age of Western culture, perhaps the very epitome of a Christian in this post-Christian era. She does not reject the Compsons, and God knows she has good reasons to do so. Unlike Ivan Karamazov, she does not give her ticket back, though it is plain that she, too, would have made Yoknapatawpha County differently. Nor does she rebel against the aspect of the Christian tradition which has fashioned Yoknapatawpha County and brought the Compsons to their present predicament. In this respect, not Dilsey, but Jason more accurately typifies many contemporaries for whom Western culture has definitely aborted and who see no exit but toward the asylum or the museum or the hinterland or folklore.

What a difference between the logic of Dilsey's existence and that of Jason's! She could not possibly subscribe to the latter's declaration, when he says: "I went on to the street, but they were out of sight. And there I was, without any hat, looking like I was crazy too. Like a man would naturally think, one of them is crazy and another one drowned himself and the other one was turned out into the street by her husband, what's the reason the rest of them are not crazy too. All the time I could see them watching me like a hawk, waiting for a chance to say Well I'm not surprised I expected it all the time the whole family is crazy."[13]

By contrast with this contrived, reluctant declaration of solidarity among men, Dilsey's is equally realistic but without the tone of unconditional surrender. For her, the task of existence is fulfilled neither through resignation nor through defiance, without implying that her mode of being is therefore an edulcorated one. On the contrary, while it is true that it stems from her Christian conviction, one must also acknowledge that objectively it embodies a simpler and, hence, a fuller insight into the human condition: we are doomed neither to solidarity nor by it, though we are all in the same boat.

"Reckin so," Luster said, "Dese is funny folks. Glad I aint none of em."

"Aint none of who?" Dilsey said. "Lemme tell you somethin, nigger boy, you got jes es much Compson devilment in you es any of em...."[14]

In and through Dilsey, beyond the sound and the fury, beyond the disfigurement of the human race, beyond the consumption and collapse of the Christian tradition, slowly but firmly rises a presence against which no human vicissitude can prevail and for which no human sorrow is too vile or decadent to bear and transfigure. A transparent rock of faith, Dilsey is the incarnation of human dignity and solicitude, almost tangibly there and yet unobtrusively available to all. In the world but not of the world. "Death is behind" her.

His name's Benjy now, Caddy said.

How come it is, Dilsey said. He aint wore out the name he was born with yet, is he.

Benjamin came out of the bible, Caddy said. It's a better name for him than Maury was.

How come it is, Dilsey said.

Huh, Dilsey said. Name aint going to help him. Hurt him, neither. Folks dont have no luck, changing names. My name been Dilsey since fore I could remember and it be Dilsey when they's long forgot me.

How will they know it's Dilsey, when it's long forgot, Dilsey, Caddy said.

It'll be in the Book, honey, Dilsey said. Writ out.

Can you read it, Caddy said.

Wont have to, Dilsey said. They'll read it for me. All I got to do is say Ise here."[15]

Here at the end, because she is here at the beginning, from first to last. One cannot help, against the background of decay and irresponsibility, from stressing the full force of Dilsey's statement, "Ise here." Indeed, with a minimum of emphasis on Faulkner's part, the ultimate significance of these words is corroborated, and the uniqueness of Dilsey's presence indicated as a cipher of the novel by the fact that for her there is no "obituary" in the appendix. Rather, her name is followed by the words, "They endured," typographically set in such a way that the reader would apply them to the Negroes and possibly the Compsons, all of them ultimately redeemed by Dilsey's mediatory presence.

Naturally, it is possible to center *The Sound and the Fury* on characters other than Dilsey or on various other themes. Faulkner himself has said that it is the story of what happens to Caddy and Quentin. Besides Benjy as a Christ-figure, one can also read the novel, as Claude-Edmonde Magny[16] suggests, along the theme of a pre-redemption hope—from a pre-Christian perspective, as it were, rather than from a post-Christian one, as we are suggesting. Or more simply, but also more narrowly, one can reduce everything to the much used and abused theme of original sin.

Sartre[17] was quite bold and original in his short essay on *The Sound and the Fury,* when he declared that time was the hero. Reflections about the meaning of time doubtless abound in a great number of passages, in the Quentin section, in particular. But quite aside from Sartre's interpretation and its compelling rigor, the problem of time in *The Sound and the Fury* must be considered, if only because of the magnificent quality of Faulkner's insights into the temporal nature of man. "Father said a man is the sum of his misfortunes. One day you'd think misfortune would get tired, but then time is your misfortune Father said. A gull on an invisible wire attached through space dragged."[18] And these words by Quentin bridging, across the ages, Saint Augustine and Sartre's existentialism: "A quarter hour yet. And then I'll not be. The peacefullest words. *Non fui. Sum. Fui. Non sum.* Somewhere I heard bells once. Mississippi or Massachusetts. I was. I am not . . . I am . . . I was not."[19]

Man is that being which becomes neither that which he is nor that which he ought to be, but that which he is not. He is, as Sartre was to write later in *Being and Nothingness,*[20] that which he is not and is not that which he is. And time itself is not until it was. But the business of time is precisely to postpone time until it was, to postpone the time when it is not, quite like the way in which Kierkegaard describes the irremediable nature of the "sickness unto death" that is despair. Faulkner himself writes, "there is nothing else in the world its not despair until time its not even time until it was."[21]

Time will not redeem man from his misfortune, nor will it redeem itself in becoming man's misfortune. In other words, existence is not self-authenticating. Is this not what Faulkner implies, when most of this novel's characters run against time, run out of time in a desperate effort to assert and authenticate themselves? Obviously, Quentin did not heed the words his grandfather told him when he gave him the watch: "I give it to you not that you may remember time, but that you might forget it now and then for a moment and not spend all your breath trying to conquer it. Because no battle is ever won he said. They are not even fought. The field only reveals to man his own folly and despair, and victory is an illusion of philosophers and fools."[22] Doubtless, time is man's misfortune.

But there is time and time, so that the impression of resignation and bondage to time scored by this exhortation calls for a correction; we must not confuse temporality and chronology. Does not Faulkner himself all too plainly warn us against that, if only by the absence of chronological sequence so emphatically characteristic of the novel? Not time so much as its facsimile, the timetable, is man's misfortune—routine, automated existence. When time looks like a schedule, then temporal existence surely does become a curse from which to flee without ever winning the victory even through suicide. Quentin realizes this when he says: "Because Father said clocks slay time. He said time is dead as long as it is being clicked off by little wheels; only when the clock stops does time come to life."[23] Which amounts to saying that being, the new being, is when time has come to life. But how does time come to life?

Easter is how the clock stops and time comes to life. Admittedly, it is difficult for modern man to realize this; our incapacity for such a reality is almost insuperable, above all because of our subjection, our blind submissiveness to the modern technological world view. But if Joshua could stop the sun, was it not because in his contemporaries' world view the universe was not a self-winding clock? The important thing is not whether Joshua actually stopped the sun, but the human stance that such an image evokes. But we are no longer capable of grasping the human reality from any similar vantage point. The substitution of an immanentist world view for a transcendental one and the atrophy of the sacral dimension of existence have resulted in the conception of time as deterministic routine, or of life as "governed" by luck.

It is because time and "luck cant do him no harm"[24] that Benjy can live out time come to life. And his life is not measured by the clicking away of seconds, of minutes, hours, and days. His chronological, "man-made" clock has stopped; past and present are mixed up, at least in appearance. What Benjy lives is the fullness of time. He does not merely recollect but smells past events, and all around him the present participates in the significance of a past event, much in the same sense, one might add, as the symbol participates in the reality of that which is symbolized. Past events are not merely recollected; through Benjy, they are also re-presented, made present again.

To borrow the German distinction, what we perceive in the case of Benjy is the unfolding of time into *Geschichte* rather than into *Historie*. As a series of facts from birth to death, the human reality belongs to *Historie*. As existing reality, however, man belongs to *Geschichte*. From the standpoint of *Historie* man appears as a chronological, or even statistical, reality. But from the standpoint of *Geschichte*, he evinces the full dimension of his temporality; he is all the facts of his life, the quantitative sum total of what took place between his birth and his death and *something more* that, being qualitative, remains irreducible.

All men are mortal—differently. If I am what I am because I remain faithful to an original decision, still each subsequent choice and the decision that follows is also a unique and original event. In *The Sound and the Fury*, Faulkner's technique makes the past present again, not in order to suggest any kind of bondage to it but to stress, as Benjy and the Easter sermon make plain, that the present always contains a new possibility, that it always offers a new choice, that it calls us to a new decision, because it opens on the future. Man, in other words, is a transcendental being. Time can be redeemed even from the routine that holds it in leash or from the chronic waste that leads to a dead end.

Not time, but eternity is the subject of *The Sound and*

the Fury. In this novel, we do not attend the disintegration of empirical existence, the cankerous corruption of generations fated to an ineluctable impasse. We attend a mystery, the mystery of being, something that transcends the clicking of seconds, the bondage of time and space, so that in the saga of Yoknapatawpha County we discern a history of the "City of God" in modern dress. What Augustine did for the Roman Empire, Faulkner does for the collapse of Constantinian Christendom, which is perceptibly giving way to a post-Christian culture. And if Faulkner's vision seems to us more tragic, it is because it originates in the death of God—in the death of one Christian cultural conception of God among others—whereas Augustine's presupposed the death of the Graeco-Roman pantheon.

The sermon, or more precisely, the Negro service is the capital event that helps us to substantiate this claim. To many readers, the sermon probably sounds like one more recapitulation of a once popular legend. Legend it is, but it plays in *The Sound and the Fury* the same rôle as the legend of the Grand Inquisitor in Dostoevski's *The Brothers Karamazov*. And, furthermore, it is a legend in the etymological sense of the term. That is to say, it tells us the meaning of the various signs and symbols as on a geographical map; it tells us how to read the drama, how to interpret the characters of the plot that has been unfolding before us. And even as, in the New Testament, Easter is the legend of Good Friday, so is the sermon the legend of *The Sound and the Fury*. As Easter comes after Good Friday, so does the sermon, an Easter sermon, come after the final dereliction of the Compsons, when man's attempts to save himself, to authenticate himself have foundered, irretrievably. And just as Good Friday reveals its meaning only in the light of Easter, so also the folly and the doom of those who attempt to conquer time, in the light of the sermon, take an another meaning.

Is it then all simply a question of perspective? Of course, it is. What existential adventure isn't? But the question is to find the perspective that best fits the destiny of man; this implies, in other words, that the meaning of existence lies outside existence, or that existence is not self-authenticating and that the fullness of time is a possibility even within time. Eternity does not "begin" after time; it happens within time. The resurrection does not take place after one's physical death; it is the only experience by which here and now the human reality can be transfigured, by which man can become that which he is not; it is the possibility of authentic existence. "I sees . . . I sees hit . . ." the minister says. "I sees de doom crack en hears de golden horns shoutin down the glory, en de arisen dead whut got de blood en de ricklickshun of the Lamb."[25] All in the present tense, that of the presence of eternity, when the clock stops and time comes to life, when all things are made new again and existence ceases to be a problem and becomes again a mystery, that is to say, a sacrament, a miracle (the Latin *sacramentum* is the translation of the Greek *mysterion*).

Existence remains a mystery even when everything has been disclosed from beginning to end. "I've seed de first en de last," Dilsey said. "I seed de biginnin en now I seed de endin."[26] What Dilsey sees is the "smashing of all human standards and evaluations"[27] by which we abdicate existence and end where the Compsons have ended. What she sees is that existence cannot be construed as "a terminated occurrence but that it is what it is only by constantly occurring anew,"[28] just like revelation and the act of faith by which revelation is grasped. Dilsey is the real iconoclast, not the Compsons, because she is the only one for whom life is an act of faith and bursts through the convenient standards and values of morality or the lack of it.

We are doubtless somewhat shocked by these declarations, if we are not in fact ready to dismiss them right off. No doubt, they sound unbelievable, much as the visiting minister did when he began to preach sounding like a white man, and Frony whispers: "En dey brung dat all de way fum Saint Looey."[29] Justifiable as her skepticism might have been, it still reminds us of Nathanael's, who exclaims: "Can anything good come from Nazareth?" to which Philip replies: "Come and see."[30] Dilsey herself, likewise, hastens to remark to Frony: "I've knowed de Lawd to use cuiser tools dan dat."[31] She knows that no sinner is too destitute to be saved, that no human being is so despicable as to deny by himself his fundamental humanity. She knows, also, that God's intervention in history is not necessarily accompanied by apocalyptic suspensions of the normal course of nature, of time; that the transcendental presence of God in the immanence of the human reality does not violate the latter's independence but manifests itself in and through it. This is why Kierkegaard identified the Christ-event, the manifestation of God's presence in Christ, as the incognito of God. On the other hand, human existence remains a mystery even while it stands revealed to itself.

It is in this light that one must listen to the sermon. Slowly, it becomes the eschatological manifestation it was meant to be. The man from Saint Looey is the herald of a new reality transfiguring the old aeon: the clock stops and God's judgment is the instrument of his mercy. And time is the time of God's patience, of God's mercy. To quote Dilsey again, speaking now to Quentin: "Dont you be skeered, honey, I'se right here."[32] All the time she has been right here. Everywhere is for her the right place. All time is for her the right time, because it is God's own time.

How can we know this?

"You'll know in the Lawd's own time." . . .
"When is the Lawd's own time, Dilsey." Caddy said.
"It's Sunday." Quentin said.[33]

It's Sunday, the day of man's rendez-vous with existence: he can miss it, but God does not; man can miss his destiny and time run out on him, but he will not miss

God, nor does the day of God's patience run out on man. Sunday is the day on which Easter is commemorated, the day of rest when the groaning of the creation ceases and man here and now becomes a new creature. It is the first and the last of the week, the beginning and the end; the birthday of man, when the old man dies and becomes a new man.

The Sound and the Fury, or foolishness to the Greeks and a scandal to the Jews, is a novel the action of which takes place in the framework of Eastertide. Without the climax it reaches in the Easter service, it is a novel about the degradation and rottenness of man. In the light of the sermon, re-enacting, re-presenting God's vindication of man's destiny, *The Sound and the Fury* affirms the possibility of a new beginning, even when the end of the rope seems to have been reached, when there seems to be no exit. Hell is other people, Sartre declares. Hell is god, Lagerkvist seems to insinuate. From Faulkner's vantage point, hell is oneself. That is to say, hell is god or other people only when they are sought as crutches. And hell is oneself, when one becomes a pair of blind crutches trying to help another across life, in vain. No pair of crutches is a good substitute for an act of faith.

How can we know this, and verify it? To be sure, we do not know this kind of reality as we know objective facts, as we acquire objective, measurable certainties. Nor is Faulkner inviting us to commit ourselves to any blind faith. History is too human both to yield any kind of certainty and to justify any kind of blind, fatalistic, or superstitious belief. Faulkner is more cautious than Camus, who wrote in *The Myth of Sisyphus*: "Between history and the eternal I have chosen history because I like certainties." [34]

Certainties may be indulged in only if it is claimed that one's knowledge is established beyond doubt, beyond any dispute. Against such allegations, Faulkner raises one question: "How can a man be expected to know even enough to doubt?"[35]

III.
The Best Possible World

✳✳✳✳✳✳✳✳✳✳✳✳✳✳✳✳✳✳✳✳✳✳✳✳✳✳

Gesang ist Dasein. ...

In Wahrheit singen, ist ein andrer Hauch.
Ein Hauch um nichts. Ein Wehn im Gott. Ein Wind.

RAINER MARIA RILKE[1]

T. S. ELIOT:
Experience Without Meaning

****

THE successive metamorphoses of our tradition and our theories of aesthetics have so altered our conception of literature that we are at pains to trace it back to its fountainhead. Poetry in particular has been one of the areas most affected by the divorce between religion and culture. The roots of this divorce extend far back into Christian times, when both sacramentarianism and otherworldliness, despite their apparent antithetical premises, were already disjoining culture from religion, though from a Christian point of view they must be neither confused nor separated. And with the advent of the modern period, the rise of secularism has further aggravated the cleavage that denatures them.[1]

In 1922, the publication of T. S. Eliot's *The Waste*

Land ushered in a new quest in literature for the meaning of existence and destiny. Unwaveringly, Eliot's poem called into question the former patterns of poetic inspiration. With the sense of an impending doom, it screened the beliefs of a literary tradition that had complacently separated itself from God and betrayed man. Reacting against this, Eliot's poetry set down the energetic framework for a new evaluation of man's condition and a new exploration of the human reality. After an age that had romantically delighted in the "unbelief" of man's natural goodness, Eliot, and others with him, reached the conclusion that the one thing common to all men was original sin.

A few years earlier, Karl Barth,[2] accomplishing a similar revolution in religious thought, had recovered, at least for Protestant theology, the fundamental doctrine of justification by faith. Eliot's rediscovery of all men's solidarity in sin attempted a bold intrusion of religion into literature in order to overcome their discord. It was a pity, however, that this had to be done by means of the dogma of original sin. That dogma is not so essential to biblical thought as is the affirmation of the ineffaceable if corruptible goodness of God's creation. Even in the depths of human depravity, biblical thought starts with this affirmation instead of that dogma. Its initial statement concerns man's original goodness and not his original sin. Hence, not man's dereliction, but man's preservation is what gives biblical thought its distinctiveness and authenticates its insight into the nature of created reality.

In spite of their common grounding in biblical thought, Barth and Eliot stand in opposition to one another. Once they have concurred on the relevance of biblical thought to man's self-understanding today, they move in different directions. Nevertheless, the relative simultaneity of their rediscoveries underlines a significant aspect of the spiritual problem of our time by characterizing the immanentism that typifies the conjuncture of modern man, as well as by shedding light on the biblical assertion that God does not bend his faithfulness to man. Thus, in their polarity, these rediscoveries (once assessed in theological language) can be said to deal with the question of God's revealedness in an age that has stripped him of his divinity and with its corollary, the hiddenness of God who humbles himself to lie speechless in the words of man.

It should be noted that this new approach to literature did not originate with Eliot. Although it was he who, by investing it with his magisterial rhythm, was heard and followed, historically it was T. E. Hulme who inaugurated this new trend. Hulme's castigation of anthropocentric humanism, incidentally, presents a strikingly Barthian atmosphere of thought in its categorical refusal to compromise: "I hold the religious conceptions of values to be right, the humanist wrong." In the midst of universal fascination with progress, Hulme did not fear bluntly to affirm his acceptance of "dogmas like that of Original Sin, which are the closest expression of the categories of the religious attitude."[3]

The enticing question that comes to mind is whether

this return to a supposedly "unenlightened" religious doctrine about man may not be merely the result of a disappointment in the idealistic optimism of Rousseau's man, rather than a rediscovery of the evangelic warning that man does not live by bread alone, let alone by optimism and progress. In view of this and other recent disenchantments, might it not be that the religious tropism of literature has been merely an attempt to quench the perennial thirst, and console the yearning, of a cult for an unknown God?

In many instances, this is undoubtedly the case. In poetry, Eliot and Auden, however, seem to be two valid and compelling exceptions. Each in his own way recaptures the fundamental qualities of the biblical image of man. Eliot's more sedate way strikes a note altogether different from the quasi-dogmatic and impulsive pronouncements of Auden. But Auden is more likely to startle and convince the secularist with his religious irony (while abashing, with his ironic religion, the secluded theologian who expects from literature nothing, or a tolerated entertainment at most).

Eliot's understanding of man's predicament forced him, like Hulme, to excoriate the humanistic forfeiture of man; injustice and evil inclinations spring from the same fountain to which humanism had assigned only the lofty aspirations of men. In Hulme's view, man is not a "well" full of infinite possibilities, but a "bucket" of finite and creaturely possibilities.

But the deification of man was not wholly the work of

arrogant optimism or sentimental, confident, and diluted spiritualism. In no small part, it was also the work of those religious views of man which had failed to recognize (as Barth, quoting Kierkegaard, reminded his generation) the infinite qualitative difference between time and eternity, and which had introduced "into human things the perfection that properly belongs only to the divine, and thus confuse[d] both human and divine things by not clearly separating them."[4] Indeed, opposition to the perfectionistic view of human nature and capabilities comes from nowhere so radically as from the biblical view of man. Man is finite and limited over against God's infinitude.

The point of departure of Eliot's mature poetry is thus a dramatic apprehension of the gap between the creature and the transcendent. No consciousness of man's true condition makes any sense, unless it stems from such an apprehension. Unfortunately, Eliot swerves from this line of thought almost immediately. For him, man "can only accomplish anything of value by discipline—ethical and political. Order is not merely negative, but creative and liberating. Institutions are necessary."[5] This admirably describes Eliot's insistent preoccupation with tradition and the orthodox institutions that transmit it.

While he makes ample room for individual personality, Eliot finds, except for mystics and those who both deny themselves and renounce the world, the main criterion of personality in the individual's subordination to society. One must bear in mind that this subordination is viewed from the same perspective that subjugates the natural to the supernatural, this world to the next, and is *ipso facto* contemptuous of this world. A certain sacramentarianism, expressive of law and order, discipline and institutions, sin and its removal, thus pervades this neo-Thomistic outlook, which the austere Eliot of Anglo-Catholicism, presumably, has borrowed from Jacques Maritain. "With the disappearance of the idea of Original Sin," wrote Eliot in *After Strange Gods*, "with the disappearance of the idea of intense moral struggle, the human beings presented to us both in poetry and prose fiction, and more patently among the serious writers than in the underworld of letters, tend to become less and less real."[6]

But it makes a difference whether one's understanding of man is renovated on the basis of the concept of original sin or in the light of the more genuine concept of the *justitia originis*, that is, the original uniqueness of man in the order of creation. Let us say that his difference is the same as that between the sacramentarian dualism of sacred and secular, on the one hand, and the charismatic compenetration or interdependence of faith and secularity, on the other. Because of an overabundance of sighing otherworldliness, Eliot misunderstands the centrifugal movement of faith and its world-facing dynamism.

Not that his poetry harbors only contempt and disparagement for the groaning and dishevelment of the creation. Like the "Virginia" piece of his *Landscapes*, some of his verse is certainly a tribute to the beauty of the creation; but we find this mostly in his minor poetry. On the whole, Eliot's preoccupation with original sin and order causes him to lose patience with human things. His general tendency is to face away from the creation. As R. A. Scott-James has aptly remarked, "He excels by introducing us to our generation, and appears to end by inviting us to turn our backs on it. It is as if the only excuse for living is that it is an opportunity for dying."[7]

A feeling of futility pervades the whole atmosphere of Eliot's apprehension of the world, the sole usefulness of it being that it affords a preparation for the world to come. This strange attitude is commanded by the same ideal that prompts Celia to say in *The Cocktail Party*:

> ... There is nothing else to do
> That is the only reason.[8]

Burdened with otherworldliness, Eliot's poetry denies the intrinsic worth of this world by approaching it as something contaminated by lust or, like dust, unbridled. In *The Confidential Clerk*, Colby says:

> Now that I have abandoned my illusions
>   and ambitions
> All that's left is love.[9]

Surely, the choice is not too flattering if Christianity is to be advocated as the only solution because all the others have failed. And why should one abandon illusions and ambitions? There must certainly be a better reason than that they come natural to man. Significantly, Eliot writes in his *Selected Essays*: "The Question is, the first question, *not* what comes natural or what comes easy to us but what is right? Either one attitude is better than the other or else it is indifferent."[10] Such an exclusive concern about what is right may reveal Eliot's affinity with the early Christians' obsession with the *regula fidei*. But it leaves little room for the glorious liberty that springs from faith. Nor would it be difficult to show that those who have been concerned with truth rather than with the right thing have also been more human, even if, like Pascal, Kierkegaard, or Dostoevski, they advocate all or nothing, a total commitment to one or the other. Could it be that Eliot is as suspicious of, or let us say skeptical about, truth as he is distrustful of what comes naturally? And yet, as he knew when he wrote "The Hippopotamus," truth has a strange way of coming naturally, just as nature has an ironic way of telling the truth. Actually, Eliot was much more human in *The Waste Land* than he has been ever since he became the poet laureate of the Church. And much more truthful, too, when he was naming, and thereby redeeming, the disillusioned and dessicated decadence of "the waste land":

                    I sat upon the shore
Fishing, with the arid plain behind me
Shall I at least set my lands in order?
London Bridge is falling down falling down
        falling down
Poi s'ascose nel foco che gli affina
Quando fiam uti chelidon—O swallow swallow
Le Prince d'Aquitaine à la tour abolie
These fragments I have shored against my ruins
Why then Ile fit you. Hieronymo's mad againe.
Datta. Dayadhvam. Damyata
        Shantih shantih shantih[11]

Where is the common ground between the peace that
passes understanding (shantih) and what is proper and
right? Eliot became a Christian and since then he has
seemed unable ever to let his hair down, even in the
company of those empty people whom he stigmatizes
for the vacuity of their purposes:

"What shall I do now? What shall I do?"
"I shall rush out as I am, and walk the street
With my hair down, so. What shall we do tomorow?
What shall we ever do?"
                    The hot water at ten.
And if it rains, a closed car at four.
And we shall play a game of chess,
Pressing lidless eyes and waiting for a knock upon
        the door.[12]

The Christian Eliot cannot tolerate the creaturely, unless it be abnegated. He cannot conceive of the transcending presence of God as honoring and transforming the world, as creative of a world and a life worth affirming. And yet exactly this is the significance of the New Testament symbol of the incarnation, which he has otherwise woven into the texture of his poetry. The incarnation means God's proximity to man, his presentness to all that is created. It means that God does not turn his back on this world, and that man must not either. Instead, articulating a mystic's flight from the world, Eliot proclaims that "the soul cannot be possessed of the divine union, until it has divested itself of the love of created beings."[13] How could Christianity forsake and at the same time penetrate the secular in order to act as a cultural leaven in it?

Once again, Eliot's intelligence of man's predicament was more genuine in *The Waste Land* than is evidenced in the private liturgical arsenal of "Ash Wednesday," or in the alternation of affirmation and denial that flows through the lines of *Four Quartets*. It is as if his justifiable rejection of the pseudohumanistic apotheosis of man were now, unjustifiably, hindering him from acknowledging that the Word become flesh lies speechless in the very words of man, or that the majesty of God assumes nothing less than both the fallen reality and intrinsic goodness of the world. What can be the reason for this discrepancy that mars Eliot's outlook and, in some measure, paralyzes his poetry by deflecting its orientation toward a sacramentarian asceticism of otherworldliness?

The real foundation of Eliot's esoteric otherworldliness may be the conscious feeling that Christianity failed to transvaluate the ephemeral values of this world, and that consequently one had better declare the world unworthy of being the theater of God's glory. As in dualistic sacramentarianism, a line of demarcation divides the Church from the world and, by implication, religion from culture. The Church must therefore collide with the world. But can we see in Eliot's argument any reason why this should happen other than that the Church is reactionary and that, having lost her relevance to the world by default, she seeks consolation for turning her back on it, instead of coming to grips with the radical immanentism by which men live today? Certainly, as Eliot himself says in *Thoughts after Lambeth*, "there is no good in making Christianity easy and pleasant."[14] Still, it must be relevant to Western culture or else acknowledge its expropriation. Of course, "we must not confound the history of a Church with its spiritual meaning. . . . A Church is to be judged by its intellectual fruits, by its influence on the sensibility of the most sensitive and on the intellect of the most intelligent, and it must be made real to the eye by monuments of artistic merit."[15] Nevertheless, what constitutes the apex of these *Thoughts* is again that otherworldly asceticism that enables Eliot to overlook the real issue, namely, the dishabilitation of the Christian tradition, and instead to indulge in some rather overzealous prognostication regarding its vitality. For example: "The World is trying the experiment of attempting to form a civilized but non-Christian mentality. The experiment will fail; but we must be very patient in awaiting its collapse; meanwhile redeeming the time; so that the faith may be preserved alive through the dark ages before us; to renew and rebuild civilization, and save the World from suicide."[16] Let us save the world, but first let it drop dead.

Eliot constantly strives to define the worth of created things in proportion as it is good for the Church. But what if the Church herself is weak? What if the decay of the world has not spared even her members?

In *Murder in the Cathedral*, Eliot himself underlines with poignancy the possibility that the weakness of the Church might not soon enough stop the decay of Western culture. But he clearly suggests also that this danger is to be blamed on the intrusion of the secular into the domestic responsibilities of the spiritual; and that, consequently, the urgent task is for the spiritual to defeat the secular, even through martyrdom—if there should be no other spectacular way. Surely, the spiritual is not always threatened from outside only. And to direct the remaining virile forces of Christianity—self-righteously?—against the secular, when all is said and done, may well be

> the greatest treason:
> To do the right thing for the wrong reason.[17]

Eliot knew this when he wrote *The Waste Land*. He knew then that even the spiritual is not immune from degeneration and decadence, and that Christian symbols too are apt to become petrified and obsolete:

> There is the empty chapel, only the wind's home
> It has no windows, and the door swings,
> Dry bones can harm no one.
> Only a cock stood on the rooftree
> Co co rico co co rico
> In a flash of lightning. Then a damp gust
> Bringing rain.[18]

Why has the chapel become the wind's home? What makes the barren wind more inspiring than a vestigial Church? Whichever stone we turn, whatever the finding, it points to the failure of the Christian tradition; to the fact that it no longer is able to assume its own meaning through Western culture. Men—including Christians—will worship idols, will worship gods (those of race, of culture or of the creeds) even while they worship God in

> an age of moderate virtue
> And of moderate vice
> When men will not lay down the Cross
> Because they will never assume it.[19]

Stemming from a dualistic understanding of man

and the universe the incarnation thus serves to stress the abyss that separates and shelters Christianity from a world bound to perish:

> The right time and the right place are not here
> No place of grace for those who avoid the face.[20]

It has happened before and it happens with Eliot that the incarnation is interpreted in such a way that it stresses an arid dichotomy between sacred and secular, and (perhaps unwittingly) fosters the spirit of secularism. At all events, the biblical meaning of the incarnation is simply being reversed so long as the least allegation is made that God's assumption of human finitude sanctions a kind of religio-cultural segregationism, instead of pointing to every man's inseparability from God's presence, even if that presence is so stifling, so doubtful, that it is abysmally felt as an absence. God never decries his creation, though it has turned away and is adulterated. By contrast, Eliot's understanding of the incarnation is, so to speak, a poetic meditation on, a reproduction of the medieval tympanum that sanctioned the cleavage between sacred and secular, this world and the next, the elect and the damned:

> Though you forget the way to the Temple,
> There is one who remembers the way to your door:
> Life you may evade, but Death you shall not.
> You shall not deny the Stranger.[21]

Neither the incarnation nor the historical translation of its reintegrating motif corroborates any longer the polarity between God and man, but is transmuted into mystical patterns of purgation. Instead of the paradoxical tension, which does not abrogate the infinite qualitative difference between God and man and yet points to their reciprocity, intensity now informs the nature of communion with God, achieved through catharsis:

> Love is most nearly itself
> When here and now cease to matter.
> ... ...
> We must be still and still moving
> Into another intensity
> For a further union, a deeper communion.[22]

Unless it is because the right time and the right place are not here, and because as soon as they concur they must be adulterated, why, indeed, should a deeper communion with God require that "here and now cease to matter"? Is man to renounce himself because he is finite? In the light of the biblical notion of the image of God in which he is created, man is finite because he can accept himself, and only thus can he then transcend his finitude. Nor can the chasm between this life and the next be bridged by renouncing this life. Creation and defilement are definitely not synonymous.

The Manichaean dualism that sustains Eliot's poetry also impregnates his Pelagian perfectionism, and neither

Manichaeism nor perfectionism accepts the relative poverty of the creation as an authentic sign of its intrinsic goodness. For neither understands that in biblical thought goodness is not quantitative, but always a relational quality. This is the reason biblical thought avoids dualism (and, by the same token, monism), whereas Eliot's world view originates in a dualistic philosophy:

> The lot of man is ceaseless labour,
> Or ceaseless idleness, which is still harder
> Or irregular labour, which is not pleasant.
> ... ...
> I say to you: *Make perfect your will.*
> I say: take no thought of the harvest,
> But only of proper sowing.
>
> The world turns and the world changes,
>
> But one thing does not change.
> In all of my years, one thing does not change.
> However you disguise it, this thing does not
>   change:
> The perpetual struggle of Good and Evil.[23]

Not that renunciation is not a virtue, but at least, it should be virile.

Was there not more religious as well as poetic virility in *The Waste Land* than there is in his religious verse? Take, for example, the opening of *The Waste Land*

and the last lines of "Journey of the Magi": In spite of their common theme, *i.e.*, the desire for death (also expressed in the epigraph to *The Waste Land*), the two poems differ considerably in tone as well as in their existential intelligence of the human predicament. It is as if Eliot's conversion had justified the reasons that connived to tempt him into being tired of this world. In *The Waste Land* authentic existence does not depend on man's consciousness of his failure, nor is it brought about by cultivating virtues. In this regard, sin makes all of us equals, as Eliot's quotation from Baudelaire indicates. Authentic existence depends on God's faithfulness, and this needs no spiritual exercise that might prove it. The immediacy of God's presence not only transcends but reintegrates the broken pieces of man's image and transforms the very possibility of disillusionment into a self-acceptance attuned to the melody of the creation:

> ... The boat responded
> Gaily, to the hand expert with sail and oar
> The sea was calm, your heart would have responded
> Gaily, when invited, beating obedient
> To controlling hands.[24]

How grim by contrast is the note on which ends the journey of the Magi in Eliot's poem! The incarnation has made their kingdoms desolate, while estranging them from their fellow men. The poem demonstrates what Eliot has already misunderstood—that the paradox of God's visitation through the incognito of the Christ-event is not to be mistaken for the reconciliation of opposites in terms of which the mystical soul asserts the reality of God by smuggling away that of the world:

> All this was a long time ago, I remember,
> And I would do it again, but set down
> This set down
> This: were we led all that way for
> Birth or Death? There was Birth, certainly,
> We had evidence and no doubt. I had seen birth
>   and death,
> But had thought they were different; this Birth was
> Hard and bitter agony for us, like Death, our death.
> We returned to our places, these Kingdoms,
> But no longer at ease here, in the old dispensation,
> With an alien people clutching their gods.
> I should be glad of another death.[25]

In his *Notes Towards the Definition of Culture*, published in 1949, Eliot observes that culture is the incarnation of a people's religion.[26] Does this mean that only one type of culture can incarnate a given religion? Or does it mean simply that culture is a more or less accurate expression of certain fundamental religious assumptions, regardless of whether these are organized into dogmas and institutions or diffusedly scattered across some collective unconscious? Either way, it is evident that, for all his professed orthodoxy, Eliot reduces Christianity to mere religiosity, the principal function of which is a utilitarian one. Religion, in other words, is the ultimate cure for all diseases, social as well as personal. "I prayed myself slim," proclaims the title of a recent book.

Indeed, upon considering that Christianity might disappear and give way to another religion, Eliot wrote: "That would not be evidence that the new religion was true, and that Christianity was false. It would merely prove that any religion, while it lasts, and on its own level, gives an apparent meaning to life, provides the framework for a culture, and protects the mass of humanity from boredom and despair."[27] Like Marx or Freud, Feuerbach had summed all this up in a straightforward and lapidary statement: *"Der Mensch ist was er isst."*[28]

But we have not been concerned here with the utilitarian aspect of religion. (Nor do we imply any denial of it.) Rather, we have been concerned with Eliot's attachment to the Christian tradition on the one hand, and, on the other, with the fact that the incarnation constitutes the central motif of this tradition. Our criticism has therefore been that while Eliot may not be wrong in extolling the values promoted by the Christian tradition, he does not sufficiently take into account the possibility that Christianity may have exhausted itself through its own cultural realizations to the point of having become irrelevant to our present situation. Instead of admitting that this regression as well as today's cultural crisis has been caused by the deliquescence of Christianity into religiosity, he blames our culture for the failure of the Christian tradition.

Our contention is that he might have spared himself from such criticism had he grasped the fuller meaning of the incarnation. The incarnation, indeed, means not only the crisis of culture but also, above all, the crisis of religion. It means that religion is man's ultimate attempt to justify himself, and it, too, fails. The incarnation means the failure of religion—of all that by which man wants to measure his goodness, his innocence; by which he wants to authenticate himself, to become like God. Is this not, as a matter of fact, the root of Eliot's perfectionism, of his preoccupation with orthodoxy, its discipline and institutions? Should we follow him, we would collaborate with him in the building of a tower of Babel.

One does hesitate, yet one feels compelled to quote Eliot against himself:

We had the experience but missed the meaning.[29]

W. H. AUDEN:
Life and Death with Our Neighbor

✳✳✳✳✳✳✳✳✳✳✳✳✳✳✳✳✳✳✳✳✳✳✳✳✳✳✳✳✳✳

NOT unlike T. S. Eliot, W. H. Auden also revolted against the dispossessed academism of a tradition paralyzed, even orphaned, by the twilight of Christianity. As did many other poets, he too set out on journeys to witness secular nativities, guided first by Marx, then by Freud, until he encountered Reinhold Niebuhr and came home again, not without having regained what he had lost—his soul.

Whether Auden is dissecting the individual or civilization, economics or politics, his primary concern is with man's integral person, both as a member of society and as a total and unique being. More than any other contemporary poet he affirms "Everything that lives is holy." Throughout his various pilgrimages, his com-

passion for man has never diminished, and when he became a Christian, it simply acquired another dimension.
Even the most superficial reading of his poetry will immediately give the reader a clue as to the source of this
compassion: it has surged, regardless of Marx, Freud,
Niebuhr and their respective influences on him, from
an inexorable awareness that man today lives another's life and loves another's love. In life and in love,
aloneness is the price for an existence man has not
chosen: "My Dear One is mine as mirrors as lonely,"[1]
because

> Since Adam, being free to choose,
> Chose to imagine he was free
> To choose his own necessity,
> Lost in his freedom, Man pursues
> The shadow of his images.[2]

Nothing less than a change of heart could redeem
man from this pursuit without substance. Whatever the
means available, in one way or another throughout the
three stages of his development Auden has consistently
advocated the necessity of taking stock of oneself. Meanwhile, the predominantly social connotations of his early
crusades against injustice, conformity, and the insipidity
of life in general (satirically expressed by "what you
need/'S a revolution within") have given way to the
urgency of an inventory of existence in which man is
defined as an individual freely assuming the necessity
of making moral choices.

In this regard, the similarities between Auden's point of departure and Eliot's are striking. Both subscribe to the doctrine of original sin even if their respective interpretations are considerably at variance with each other. Eliot's understanding is a thoroughly "religious" one, by which we mean that it is intrinsically bound to a special system of belief. Original sin, therefore, cannot mean anything to the reader unless he too accepts the system of belief in which it makes sense. Otherwise, it fails to materialize, or the poem fails to communicate its meaning. This is the reason many of Eliot's poems, instead of incarnating, merely describe what he as a Christian thinks about the predicament of man. Eliot's understanding of original sin explains in a great measure the persistent note of expiation punctuating so many of his lines, while at the same time accounting for his perfectionistic approach to Christianity.

Auden's interpretation of original sin is free from subservience to a superannuated body of beliefs. It not only means something to the Christian who adheres to that doctrine, but also informs natural man's understanding of himself. Auden strives to bring its meaning into universal acceptance, and he succeeds, largely because this meaning is not extraneous to the poem, but fuses with it, and belongs to the very fullness of the poem, which then becomes the *kairos*, or occasion of an artistic comprehension of the human reality. Faith and art, in such a poem, cease to be heterogeneous elements, or to flirt with each other. But art has translated all the content of faith into poetry; and the religious meaning of original sin is better conveyed for being rid of its fig leaf, so to speak, and for being woven into the fabric itself of the poem:

> Recalled from the shades to be a seeing being
>   From absence to be on display,
> Without a name or history I wake
>   Between my body and the day.
>
> Holy this moment, wholly in the right,
>   As, in complete obedience
> To the light's laconic outcry, next
>   As a sheet, near as a wall,
> Out there as a mountain's poise of stone,
>   The world is present, about,
> And I know that I am, here, not alone
>   But with a world, and rejoice
> Unvexed, for the will has still to claim
>   This adjacent arm as my own,
> The memory to name me, resume
>   Its routine of praise and blame,
> And smiling to me this instant while
>   Still the day is intact, and I
> The Adam sinless in our beginning,
>   Adam still previous to any act.
>
> I draw breath; that is of course to wish
>   No matter what, to be wise,
> To be different, to die and the cost,
>   No matter how, is Paradise

Lost of course and myself owing a death:
    The eager ridge, the steady sea,
The flat roofs of the fishing village
    Still asleep in its bunny,
Though as fresh and sunny still, are not friends
    But things to hand, this ready flesh
No honest equal but my accomplice now,
    My assassin to be, and my name
Stands for my historical share of care
    For a lying self-made city,
Afraid of our living task, the dying
    Which the coming day will ask.[3]

Auden's understanding of original sin, as well as the sagacity he displays in identifying man's depravity, does not in the least result in any drab conception of humanity, but in the correct if paradoxical apprehension that man is that free being who only imagines he is free. Because man will not use but abuse his freedom, he "is not, as the romantics imagined, good by nature. Men are equal not in their capacities and virtues but in their natural bias toward evil."[4]

The difference between Eliot and Auden corroborates their different approach to the relation of religion and culture. Eliot's is ritualistic and sacramentarian; Auden's is charismatic. That is to say, the former is dominated by the idea of law and accordingly transforms the tradition into an institution, whereas the latter is dominated by the idea of grace and turns the tradition into an event of daily life. The former seeks to determine how and where to find the grace of God, whereas the latter seeks to deal with the fact that this grace comes to man and finds him where he least expects it. For this reason, Auden does not evolve any sacerdotal exclusivism from his intuition of the encounter between God and man. The right time and the right place are never to be found in the future or in any withdrawal from the world. Nor are they located within the precincts of an institutionalized and separatist community; they are to be found here and now.

This special emphasis shows that Auden's idea of original sin is (as it should be) apprehended from the perspective of the *justitia originis*, the covenantal relationship in which God and man belong together here and now. Original sin thus provides man with a knowledge of his condition that is essentially retrospective knowledge, just as it is from the standpoint of faith that sin becomes a reality and the Christian knows that he is, was, and always will be, sinful. Unlike Eliot, Auden does not preach about original sin and extol the virtues of expiation and otherworldliness. Instead, his poetry creates a world that, like God's creation, is good until it meets—and this it must—with the ambiguities of its own goodness.

In consonance with his ritualistic view of sin, furthermore, Eliot views religion as man's quest for God. Auden, on the contrary, because he begins with man's ultimate inseparability from God, reverses the terms of man's quest; instead of the known seeking the unknown, he realizes the world-facing movement of the biblical symbol of the incarnation, and that

Today the unknown seeks the known.[5]

That is the reason no trace of Manichaeism is to be found in Auden's poetry. For as long as man's quest is cast solely in terms of the known seeking the unknown, the inevitabe result is the disparagement of all that is creaturely. Neither can it ultimately heal man's essential wound, his aloneness. This is exactly what *The Age of Anxiety* corroborates: were the object to be pursued through expiation and abnegation, the quest would indeed consist in an ascent of the soul into Abraham's bosom. Only, the bosom will never be reached:

> For the new locus is never
> Hidden inside the old one
> Where reason could rout it out,
> Nor guarded by dragons in distant
> Mountains where Imagination
> Could explore it; the place of birth
> Is too obvious and near to notice,
> Some dull dogpatch a stone's throw
> Outside the walls, reserved
> For the eyes of faith to find[6]

And Abraham's bosom will never be reached because God's

> . . . Question disqualifies our quick senses,
> His Truth makes our theories historical sins,
> It is where we are wounded that is when he speaks
> Our creaturely cry, concluding His children
> In their mad unbelief to have mercy on them all
> As they wait unawares for His World to come.[7]

In keeping with the key symbol of Christianity, a symbol which implies a movement from God to man, from the transcendent to the immanent, Auden's poetry is grounded in a world-facing understanding of grace; consequently it harbors no contempt or repugnance for the ambiguous aspirations of man and the distortions of love.

> O look, look in the mirror,
>   O look in your distress;
> Life remains a blessing
>   Although you cannot bless.
>
> O stand, stand at the window
>   As the tears scald and start;
> You shall love your crooked neighbour
>   With your crooked heart.

And notwithstanding the fact that

> In headaches and in worry
> Vaguely life leaks away,[8]

"all actions and diversions of the people, their grey-
hound races, their football competitions, their clumsy
acts of love, what are they but the pitiful, maimed expressions of that entire passion, the positive tropism of
the soul to God?"[9] Under the aspect of both *eros* and
agape (perhaps of *agape* more than *eros*), love thus ir-
radiates the poetry of Auden. Even in his most erotic
verse, *agape* still constitutes the access to the meaning
of that passion of the soul, however warped and disfigured. Facing and attuned to the creation, Auden's art
carries in its most human fabric, like a reminiscence, the
rhythm and cadence of "the healing fountain" "in the
deserts of the heart." [10] Affirming and transfiguring the
world, Auden protests against the sequestration of life
and of love:

> Space is the Whom our loves are needed by,
> Time is our choice of How to love and Why.[11]

To live, hence, means to survive aloneness and the darkness that has descended upon all humanity, for

> The choice to love is open till we die
> ... ...
> O living Love replacing phantasy,
> O Joy of life revealed in Love's creation;
> Our mood of longing turns to indication.[12]

The groaning of the creation, the frustrations of life, the fragility of existence point to that absolute dependence of man by which his existence is authenticated. This absolute dependence is not a feeling but the experience of the immediacy of God's transcending presence in his creation, as expressed through the symbol of the incarnation. Therefore, here and "Now and forever we are not alone," because "the Word which is implicit in the Beginning and in the End is become immediately explicit. . . ." It follows, hence, that "having seen Him not in some prophetic vision of what might be, but with the eyes of our weakness as to what actually is, we are bold to say that we have seen our salvation."[13]

One can doubtless, in view of the foregoing, concur with Spender's judgment that "essentially the direction of Auden's poetry has been towards the defining of the concept of love,"[14] here and now, amidst the slums of man's soul, wherein "so many people try to forget their aloneness and break their heads and hearts against it."[15] And doubtless, too, it is in this sense that Auden's poetry concerns itself with God's quest for man. "The special Christian Revelation," he writes in an article for *The New Republic* (June 2, 1941), "the Incarnation, occurred precisely at that moment in history when an impasse seemed to have been reached."

God is man's destiny, or else this destiny is bound to flounder; man's quest can go only through a Garden of Eden that cannot exist, beckoned by a miracle that cannot occur, even while the self can only assert a

selfish "I," unable to "wait without idols to worship."[16]
He who rejects the world is also he who wants to reverse time to go back to some golden age, or to hasten
time in order to escape from the present; who wants to
remake the creation in order to inaugurate a universe
of discourse that has achieved logical consistency. On
the contrary, the incarnation symbolizes the fact that

The Kingdom of Heaven has come, not in our present
And not in our Future, but in the Fullness of Time.[17]

Our commentary would be incomplete if we did not
conclude with a few remarks about the task of existing
in the present context of Western culture. Modern civilization, Auden seems to claim, can be retrieved only if
the spiritual acts as a leaven in the secular, and re-
orients it toward its true destiny, where it says "thou
art" to the Wholly Other's "I am"—providing of course
the Christian tradition is still capable of assuming such
a rôle.

For the garden is the only place there is, but you
    will not find it
Until you have looked for it everywhere and found
    nowhere that is not a desert;
The miracle is the only thing that happens, but to
    you it will not be apparent,
Until all events have been studied and nothing
    happens that you cannot explain;

And life is the destiny you are bound to refuse
until you have consented to die.

Therefore, see without looking, hear without listen-
ing, breathe without asking:
The Inevitable is what will seem to happen to you
purely by chance;
The Real is what will strike you as purely absurd;
Unless you are certain you are dreaming, it is
certainly a dream of your own;
Unless you exclaim—"There must be some mistake"—you must be mistaken.[18]

The garden is no place in which to vegetate in heavenly
ecstasies. It does not call for any flight from the scenes
of human meaninglessness, or from the mass of aloneness. The whole tropism of the soul toward God manifests itself through its compassion and love for God's
creation, whereas man's ultimate concern never shuns
but hallows his more provisional, this-worldly responsibilities and obligations. Which amounts to saying, in
more terrestrial terms, that the garden is simply where

There are bills to be paid, machines to keep in
repair
Irregular verbs to learn, the Time Being to redeem
From insignificance.[19]

Therefore—and this applies to Christians as well as to
every man:

If we really want to live, we'd better start at once
    to try

If we don't, it doesn't matter, but we'd better start
    to die.[20]

SAINT-JOHN PERSE:
A Name in Which to Live

****

WHETHER or not the desacralization of Western culture was inevitable, it was certainly facilitated and even hastened not only by the Renaissance but also by the movement toward secularity that orginated in the Reformation. And yet the Reformation must be exonerated from the charge of deconsecrating Western culture. What the Reformers' understanding of faith necessitated, indeed, was not the secularization of culture but the secularization of the Christian tradition; not secularism, but secularity or the spiritualization of culture. By secularizing the Christian tradition, the Reformation aimed at a transfiguration, a consecration of culture.

What took place, instead, was the progressively successful secularization of culture dominated by a radical immanentism that was diametrically opposed to the fundamental principles of the Reformation and whose rise Protestantism—if it was at all willing—was still not able either to prevent or to restrict. Nor, for that matter, was the Counter-Reformation so geared as to avert this triumphal march of secularism and immanentism, the cultural and religious manifestation of which lies in the idea of the death of God.

Today, practical atheism has become a valid alternative to the paralysis that has been affecting the Christian faith for so long a time. But practical atheism too, though it has its virtues, is in the last analysis faced with a handicap analogous to that of Christian otherworldliness. Self-reliant and self-contained, radical immanentism is not less immune from aberrance than the most delinquent, disincarnate otherworldliness. To reverse the positions is not enough. If one evaded the world, it is not sufficient for the other to bury its head in it. Both solutions represent similar attempts on the part of man to face away from himself and, by different ways, both lead ultimately to a drastic devaluation of man. This is what André Malraux denounces when he writes: "On the whole face of the globe the civilization that has conquered it has failed to build a temple or a tomb."[1]

At the threshold of the post-Christian era our morality is still Christian but is not girded by the Christian faith. By merely eliminating the values of the Christian tradition, instead of seeking to transubstantiate them in terms of a valid immanental vision of the world, radical immanentism has only succeeded in devaluating them. It has simply contented itself with leveling them down. But it has not been able to offer an alternative basis to secure the integrity of the human reality. And yet nothing less than the dignity of man is and continues to be at stake.

Nor can we afford to be inconsistent with ourselves, whether or not the Christian faith can still act as leaven. Either we recognize the gap that severs the Christian faith from our cultural involvement, and try to close this gap, or we must seek to formulate an immanental universe of discourse in which to ground those values that until now were justified by their transcendental frame of reference. We can cheat our gods, but not man; we cannot cheat the image of God (or its equivalent in an immanentist language) in which man is created. The problem is not simply to translate but to ascribe to an immanental source those values which so far were relevant precisely because of their transcendental origin.

Such is the task that devolves upon us, if we realize the gravity of the present crisis and have rejected the Christian faith. Such a task is a cultural one, though we must also remember that every cultural activity is the adumbration of a religious *élan*, and that basically culture is a religious activity. That is why there has always been a special affinity between religion and culture. When this affinity is squandered, religion cannot restore it merely by fiat. For the converse also is true: religion is a cultural activity. One can be recognized by the other. Culture is the incorporation of the sacred element inherent in religion. But this can happen only if culture recognizes itself in the otherness represented by that sacred element.

Recognition also implies a choice. It is a choice in favor of something for which we have been prepared, toward which we tend, and yet which adds something new to our project: the more we conform, or "catch up" with our culture, the *less* we look like ourselves—we become that which we are not. Every aspect of culture presents a similar ambiguity, every culture possesses an equivocal reality that seeks to be transcended, to be transfigured. From a theological point of view, one could appropriately remark that, whereas Christianity calls for secularity, culture calls for transfiguration—a transfiguration parallel to that of the human reality in the process by which it becomes that which it is not. The new man in Christ is said to be a Christ-bearer; in the same manner, culture attests to the sacred by which it is transfigured, or which it gropes for.

Hence, the renovation needed to solve the present crisis can succeed only if it postulates the priority of a cultural reconversion. Theology is useless without the cultural tools to communicate it. So long as we do not meet the present crisis from this angle, our civilization will be able to build neither a temple nor a tomb. Most urgent, therefore, is the necessity to overcome our cultural alienation. It is from this perspective that we propose to consider the work of Saint-John Perse, who writes:

Wisdom in the foam, O plagues of the mind in the crepitation of salt and the milk of the quick-lime!

I learn a science from the soul's insurrections ... The wind tells us its piracies, the wind tells us its errors!

Like the Rider, lariat in hand, at the gate of the desert,

I watch in this vast arena signs of good omen soaring.

And morning, for our sake, moves her prophetic finger through sacred writings.

Exile is not of yesterday! exile is not of yesterday! ... "O vestiges, O premisses,"

Says the Stranger on the sands, "the whole world is new to me . . ." And the birth of his song is no less alien to him.[2]

Patiently, for fifty years or so, Perse has lent his breath to a prophetic reclaiming of this no-God's-land civilization where we seem to be stalled between signs without goals, before texts without glossaries. Perse has excelled in deciphering what seem to be hieroglyphic documents from which man attempts to wrench the meaning of existence. These long poems, which from one breathless vision to another exalt the mutual allegiance between man and the world, are so many documentaries of a creation patiently yielding the meaning of its signs. In this respect, we may take note in passing of a certain affinity between Perse and certain other poets. In spite of what seems to be a difference of spirituality, neither Perse's nor Auden's poetry reflects a world that is fatigued; and both of them stand diametrically opposed to Eliot. Through each of them poetry has matured its vocation as an instrument of transfiguration, but Eliot's approach to Western culture has been that of a theologian in the traditional sense; he belongs to the category of those who would conceive of the future of modern man as dependent upon a theological revival. In this lies the major difference between Perse and his translator Eliot. Perse rightly is aware of the priority of a cultural reconversion, whether or not it will lead to a theological renewal.

The French poet Paul Claudel also presents what can be mistaken for an affinity with Perse, because of a similarity in the structure of their language, in the rhythm of their verse; but there yawns between them an unbridgeable gap. Claudel poses. He studies what effect the cadence of the word would have on the redemption of the world. His style is baroque, and, with a few exceptions, a literary *trompe-l'oeil*, just as his metaphysical effervescence is a religious *trompe-l'oeil*. To recall the comment that Bernanos makes in *The Diary of a Country Priest*, Claudel's work makes one think of those Renaissance painters who had their mistresses pose for them to paint the Virgin.[3] The artifact is a little too apparent in Claudel's prolixity, and his poetry results in a diversion (in Pascal's sense).

Cathedrals once were Bibles hewn in stone for the instruction of the illiterate. We would say of Perse's poetry that it is a verbal monument whose purpose is to help those who no longer can discern the dimension of the sacred inherent or latent in the things and beings of this world—in the wind, in the snow and the rain, in the scattered elements of nature, in the creation in whose midst man encounters his enigmatic destiny and sinks in, or is illumined by, the mystery of his being.

Clear and hermetic, ample and compact, at a man's height, Perse's poetry revives in us the sense of the sacred, of the numinous. In many respects a litany of baptismal restoration, his work celebrates a world that is recovering its sacramental attributes, and praises the covenant that these unveil between man and the world. Springing from the things of this world and relying on them, the spiritual adventure of man can begin.

Little by little, the poetic universe of Perse reveals a design and a purpose. One presently notices that this universe constitutes nothing but the sacerdotal setting for the execution of a plan to valorize space and time, here and now, to redeem (as Auden would say) man from insignificance. The universe is a temple. Erected to the glory of no God, perhaps. Probably. But it is a temple, a sacral structure, in which is transfigured the sacramental drama of human existence.

According to the Old Testament, in order that the Ark of the Covenant may symbolize the presence of God it must remain empty: the majesty of God cannot be confined to the Ark, but transcends that through which God manifests his presence. The purpose of Perse's poetry is to express a covenant between man and the world. And the "ark" by which such a covenant is signified does not symbolize God's presence, but his absence. In Perse's universe nothing can indeed symbolize God's presence. With regard to God, only his absence can be symbolized. But the reason Perse's symbols derive their efficacy from God's absence is that they symbolize another reality— the mystery of being. This is the mystery that can be indicated and celebrated, even experienced, but not violated or denatured by being supernaturalized or hypostasized in a realm of ideas above and beyond this world. The covenant between man and the world reminds us, not of God's necessity, but of man's contingency. We must assume this contingency of man's obscure condition in order that we may transfigure it, whether heaven is gracious unto us, or not.

Like Kakfa, Perse never speaks of God. The universe that he recapitulates is a universe without God. But it is the world itself, in its objective reality, with its nonchalant weakness, its opacity and its disponibility, which makes any flight into Abraham's bosom superfluous.

> I also love my dogs, the call of my finest horse,
> and to see at the end of the straight avenue my
> cat coming out of the house accompanied by the
> monkey . . .

all things sufficient to keep me from envying the
sails of the sailing ships
which I see on a level with the tin roof on the sea
like a sky.[4]

When Perse invokes the gods, the term makes us think
of that grandeur of man of which man is not the measure, or of the indomitable forces of nature, before
which even the glory of man comes to flounder ultimately; in no way is man's grandeur here a pretext for
self-deification. On the contrary, self-deification is an
obsolete contradiction of human nature, and man's
grandeur consists in his dependence upon a reality that
is not meant to be controlled, whether it is divine or not.
Perse does not call upon our traditional notions of
divine transcendence to convince us of the contingency
of man's condition and its meaningfulness. Nor does he
advocate a thoroughgoing immanentism or extol the perfidious idea of man's self-reliant innocence. He performs the *tour de force* of transubstantiating in terms of
an immanentist universe our traditional transcendental
values.

If the temple is encumbered by money-changers, they
must be chased out. If it is littered with the dead bodies
of belief, we must let the dead bury their dead. When
a new epoch of man's destiny is dawning, we must first
cleanse the universe of the parasitic expectations that
falsify our self-understanding. Indeed, it is not so much
a question of turning our back on the past as of starting

on the right foot, of deciding which future alone is worth choosing to preserve man's integrity.

And do you not see, suddenly, that everything is crashing around us—all the masting and everything, the rigging with the main yard, and the whole sail over our faces—like a great fold of dead faith, like great folds of empty robes and false membranes—

And that at last, on deck, it is time to use the axe? . . .[5]

And yet, it is important to note that Perse's world view is based on a refusal, one could even go so far as to say, on a metaphysical rebellion. But this rebellion is not lined either with anguish or with torment, and is equally divested of that Promethean *je ne sais quoi* through which some contemporary authors probe man and the world. When Perse says "No," he does not address any supernatural order or the disfigured image of some supreme being. Rebelling neither against God nor against his creation, Perse has no ticket he might defiantly give back, like Ivan Karamazov. He says "No" to the assumption, the naïve presuppositions of a desacralized universe. He says "No" to the posture of man wallowing in postulates that are as deceptive as they are enticing. The very premise of a desacralized universe in the last analysis rests on a stillborn belief: it is to such an imposture that Perse says "No."

When he received the Nobel Prize in Stockholm, Perse himself said that the real drama of our age lies in the increasing gap that separates "temporal man" from "intemporal man." It is the responsibility of the undivided poet to testify to this twofold vocation of man, to awaken man to this vocation. And should man have forgotten that he was made of dust from the ground, the dust might remind him of his spiritual nature. In this mission consists the poet's obligation to be the bad conscience of his time.

Perse fulfills this obligation simply by avoiding the false attitudes of the rebel and of the immoralist as well as of the *bien-pensant*. Neither Anti-Christ nor Prometheus, Perse does not consider the poetic act as an attempt to re-create the world, or to correct the creation. He disavows the kind of poetic act that covertly seeks to deify man's imagination if not to substitute it for some divine creativity fancied by man. The poet is not a demiurge, nor are the works of the imagination a countercreation. The truth is that by the very nature of his spiritual adventure man is bound to the world as it is. Nor is truth itself a dogma promulgated by some demiurge or snatched from some God *manqué*, for the simple reason that though the universe is filled with gods it is neither the abode nor the footstool of God; it is the immanence of the sacred that pervades it with mystery. Supposing that God is, he would be a God *manqué*. Why then waste one's temporality on trying to become like God? The task of existing is too sacred as well as imperative to be risked on such an erroneous projection of the human reality. Man is such that he could not bear becoming like God. And if there is no God, why should man seek to deify himself?

With Perse, poetry has recovered its sacerdotal character. However, this sacerdotal function is not to be understood in terms of a vertical but in terms of a horizontal mediation. From this perspective, the poet is a priest of the word, but the incarnation of the word brings to light not only the real nature of man's estrangement but also his reconciliation with the world and himself. The poem is a celebration of this event. Truly apocalyptic, that is, revealing only that which does not violate the mystery of man's being, Perse's poetry celebrates not a divine parousia but that of man.

Thus it is that Perse restores to the universe its sacral dimension and desecularizes the world, while his poetry becomes a cosmic psalm celebrating the enthronement of man in his rightful kingdom, or sung as an introit upon the occasion of man's advent into the world or of the word incorporating that which it names. The bond between man and the world is like the bond between the word and the thing it names. This bond can be adulterated or severed, and man will then drift away from himself. It never is a label, a program, or a creed, but always a moment—the moment of adequacy between man and the world, between the word and the thing it names (and the word is as eloquent as the thing remains ineffable).

My hands more naked than at birth, and lips more free, ear to the coral reef that sounds the lament of another age,

Behold, I am restored to my native shore . . . There is no history but the soul's, no ease but the soul's.

With the achene and the anopheles, with the culm and the sands, with the frailest things, with the idlest things, the simple thing, the simple thing of here, the simple thing of being here, as day drains away . . .[6]

The central theme of Perse's work also concerns man's availability to the world and his transfiguring presence in it. This act of man's presentness to the world is also the instrument of his adherence to the world, to nature as well as to his nature, to the history and ease of the soul. "All the paths of the world eat out of his hand"[7] at the same time as man realizes "that it is strange to be there, hands plunged in the facility of day . . ."[8] For the simplicity of being, of "being there," is not the simplicity of objects, of things, but always exhibits itself as apprehended with a sense of strangeness. Adequacy and strangeness, adhering to the world and being estranged from it, indeed, spring from the same fountain; they originate in wonder, as does the act itself of existing. Only as a stranger can man be really there, at one with the world and with himself, reconciled with the history of his soul, which is nothing other than the incarnation of wonder occurring when man is there, "hands plunged in the facility of day."

To this facility of day corresponds the ease of the soul. And the dawn of day corresponds to the dawn of existence, suggesting a covenant of harmony between man and the world. But nothing is stranger than this ease of man's being there. At the very threshold of existence, man is already estranged from himself, he acts like a stranger: "Once, once I had a taste for living among men, but now earth breathes out its alien soul."[9] Alienated as soon as he crossed the threshold of existence, man must "each day pitch camp farther from [his] birthplace."[10] He must yet conquer the country of which he is a native, conquer his name, become that which he is not. *Anabasis* is the poem of this conquest.

But one cannot conquer one's past. And home is nowhere, because everywhere is a place to which one comes back. And insofar as only a stranger can be at home with others, man—this stranger—is at ease, at one with himself as though he were another. In this contingency of his destiny, man can experience the necessity of his freedom to be there.

A poem of conquest and annexation, *Anabasis* also describes man's irresistible effort to enter again into possession of his soul and into communion with the reality of the world, the itineraries of which guide the natural inclinations of the soul struck with wonder. It is not a question of gaining the world, but oneself. Nor is it a question of setting up successive empires so much as honoring and transfiguring the world. Existence is a struggle between a temporal being whose glory is ephemeral and "eternity yawning on the sands."[11] The struggle perhaps is unequal. It is better so than being unequal to oneself.

After his victorious struggle with the angel, Jacob's name was changed. He was given one in which he could live. For Perse, man changes his name for a nameless one; the conqueror becomes an exile—because his land is not ruled over by any god. The reason (we can grasp it now) God is absent from the universe of Saint-John Perse is that the concept of God would lead to the idea of an ultimate formulation, of a final definition of existence. So many believers indeed act like specialists. But the task of existing is too exigent to be entrusted to any specialist. Religion, in particular, often sublimates the ambiguities of existence for the sake of a certainty beyond dispute as well as beyond this life. There is indeed a way of "perishing from an excess of prudence,"[12] which makes God useless and man *de trop* in the universe. But, for Perse, ambiguous as the human reality may be, neither man nor the world is *de trop*.

For man is in question, and his reintegration.
Will no one in the world raise his voice? Testimony for man . . .
Let the Poet speak, and let him guide the judgment![13]

It is not without significance that the French word

rendered here by "reintegration" is *renouement*. The verb *renouer* means to tie, to bind again, to resume (a conversation) or renew (a friendship). By extension, it implies the notion of communion, of communication, of dialogue—a dialogue between *I* and *Thou*. For Perse, it suggests also an encounter between the self and the world, a covenantal bond with all that is. For this purpose, the reintegration of man necessitates the recovery of that original integrity through which he participates in the permanence and unity of being, in the mystery of being. Furthermore, one cannot *renouer* with another except insofar as one is *available*. But being available does not mean giving up the originality of one's person; nor does it mean objectifying the secret of which each person is a trustee. On the contrary, transfigured existence is like sharing a secret only to discover then that it has truly become one's own and authenticates one's presence in the world.

The poetry of Perse is a transcription of this itinerary from self to self; his poetry goes through dust and glory, and blazes the trail of man's covenant with the universe. Such is the humanism as well as the function of poetry to which Saint-John Perse remains faithful, by fathoming the mystery of being and showing us the way toward a recovery of man, of a name in which to live.

IV.
Faith, Reason, and Existence

※※※※※※※※※※※※※※※※※※※※※※※※※※

> *Nous n'avons pas assez de force pour suivre toute notre raison.*
> —La Rochefoucauld[1]

> Faith begins precisely there where reason leaves off.
> —Kierkegaard[2]

FYODOR DOSTOEVSKI:
Where Reason Leaves Off

****

ALTHOUGH the novels of Dostoevski are charged with thought, they never, as André Gide said, become abstract; they remain novels. Nor do his characters, representative as they are, ever cease being concrete people and become merely symbolic. The difficulties of life are too grave and its contradictions too particular for the kind of novelist Dostoevski was to indulge in any theoretical teaching about some abstract human nature. In point of fact, human nature is what men are and do individually. It is not indicated by their external behavior so much as sanctioned by an inward concordance with the outward manifestations of human relations; as Dostoevski said, according to Gide's quotation, "there are moments which demand to be lived correctly, and that is far more important than being on time at an appointment."[1] It is not surprising, then, that his books do not turn into mere psychological, sociological, political, or even theological treatises, but display verities that such treatises are likely to overlook. Quite simply, his aim was to transcribe the deeds and behavior by which each man is measured against his inner self, by which he questions his inner self.

The nature of this question was elucidated by Dostoevski himself, when he declared that *The Brothers Karamazov* dealt with the question from which he had suffered all his life, consciously or subconsciously: the existence of God. And it is worth emphasizing right away the particularity of his approach: the problem of God can be raised by the believer alone, not by the unbeliever; which is the main reason atheistic arguments against the existence of God inevitably miss the mark. For the problem of God is not, in Dostoevski's view, a secular, but a religious problem. Only more recently, one may add, has it become a secular problem, too, and has the drive toward radical immanentism almost succeeded in stifling the question of God and making it practically unintelligible to modern man. It is as if for the first time God no longer were our contemporary. In this connection, not the least merit of *The Brothers Karamazov* is that it anticipates modern man's inability to raise the question of God and, by compensation, his proneness to rush headlong into substitutes, whether ideological, pseudoscientific, or morbidly religious.

A comparison with *The Scarlet Letter* will perhaps clarify this matter. The world view in terms of which the action of *The Scarlet Letter* takes place, although it is not necessarily Hawthorne's own world view, is that of a harmonious universe and presupposes the notion of law and order. This is also conveyed by the feeling that things were at one time better than they are going to be when the novel has begun. The Puritan community claims to incarnate the will of God, and is a model of virtue, formally and externally at least.

Then, too, in Hawthorne's novel the universe is conceived of as obeying a definite purpose. Sin is not harmless and superfluous; it is what thwarts the purpose of the universe and must be punished and eradicated even at the cost of letting the inflexible pursuit of *summum jus* result in a *summa injuria*. Finally, in spite of all the witch-hunting and the legalistic apparatus of Puritan morality, the community still considers (theoretically, at least) innocence as a gift of God, like life itself.

But the world of *The Brothers Karamazov* does not presuppose the notion of a harmonious whole. It is as broken and dissolute as the Karamazov family. The universe is not in accord with the idea of a moral order. No purpose animates it toward any ultimate end. If anything, the world still remains to be defined and human existence to be examined—but from what vantage point? Besides, the world is incoherent—how can anyone dare to endure it innocently? No assumption of any kind is permissible and man is faced with the question: in the name of what do I live? Or, is there any virtue if there is no immortality? Ivan wants to know, as does each of the Karamazovs, each of whom in his way is improvising his answer to this question, without benefit of any prompting, let alone of any rehearsal. Or, as Paul Ramsey raises the question, "can there be morality without immortality?"[2] Can there be morality without judgment, either the Last Judgment or the judgment of others, here and now?

To make sure that we have not missed the point, Dostoevski compels us to confront the question more concretely than can be done with words like "immortality" or "Last Judgment" or "in the name of what does one live?" or even "morality." Indeed, we must come to grips with the final question, which not a single device can help existence to avoid. How, Dostoevski asks in effect, can one live without at the same time constituting oneself as a judge of others, one way or another?

Even Alyosha, who "was fond of people" and who "did not care to be a judge of others,"[3] if he does not will himself to be a judge of others, nonetheless constitutes others as judged by him. "I feel," his father says to him, "that you're the only creature in the world who has not condemned me."[4] That this is definitely one if not the fundamental aspect of the problem with which Dostoevski tortures his creatures is further indicated by Ivan's inquiry: "Brother," he tells Alyosha, "let me ask you one thing more: has any man a right to look at other men and decide which is worthy to live?"[5]

Given this perspective, we can already sense that the drama of the Karamazov family will, in the last analysis, turn out to be a sort of "little apocalypse," a literary (instead of pictorial or sculptural) *Last Judgment*. In the biblical view of the Last Judgment, what is significant is not that some are rewarded and others punished, but that there is a Judge whether our deeds have been motivated by the thought of immortality or not. And, moreover, the parable of the *Last Judgment* unambiguously implies that, whether we believe in God or not, we have no excuse for eluding the common mandate by which all men are morally obligated to and responsible for one another. Having mentioned this, we can see more clearly what Dostoevski is driving at. Indeed, though his thesis may be that there is no morality without immortality, his argument makes sense only if this does not mean that without immortality one cannot or ought not to be moral—on the contrary. That this makes morality more difficult goes without saying. It also does, however, make it more relevant, and prepares us for Dostoevski's affirmation that since the existence of God does not hinge on our morality, it depends much less on our immorality; and that there must be a Judge, whether morality is justified in the name of immortality or not; and that this Judge is not a Grand Inquisitor, but his prisoner, the bearer and instrument of God's justice, the Christ. It is mainly through Alyosha's instrumentality, although Grushenka's "legend of the onion"[6] also makes the same point, that we are brought to this view.

Like the "sheep" of Matthew XXV who are rewarded for having done the right thing but are unbelievingly surprised when the Judge declares this to them, Alyosha's morality is not what justifies his faith in God.

Clearly, Dostoevski is suggesting that neither the existence of God, nor his absence, excuses man from being moral, though perhaps man, enticed by his logic, wishes that it did. Not that for the believer there is no connection between morality or authentic existence and faith in God; or that the reality of God is superfluous to the exercise of morality. But even for the believer, practice of morality is no proof of God's existence or of immortality. The existence of God and the idea of immortality are alike a matter of faith. That is to say: though it is permissible to derive virtue from faith and lay down the foundations of morality on the assumption of God's existence, the reverse reasoning is not possible.

Strange as it may sound, is this not precisely what Ivan himself has also understood, though he does not believe it or admit it to himself? And is it not what Rakitin, too, seems to have dimly perceived, although he does not agree with Ivan and tries therefore to argue that, in the absence of God, "humanity will find in itself the power to live for virtue even without believing in immortality. It will find it in love for freedom, for equality, for fraternity"?[7] Ivan's position is of course more radical, yet not so unlike Rakitin's; both positions consist merely in seeking another basis than God for morality, or the lack of it; both Ivan and Rakitin are actually groping for another type of morality than a theonomous one. "If you were to destroy in mankind the belief in immortality," suggests Ivan, according to Miüsov's report, "nothing then would be immoral, everything would be lawful."[8]

But incisive as the logic of Ivan's argument may sound, if we examine it more closely, we discover that its trenchant style, like a prestidigitator's trick, bribes our attention away from the heart of the matter so artfully we tend to overlook what it is all about. For, what Ivan's argument actually bears out is that his very proposal of an autonomous morality, whether it works successfully or not, is predicated on the contention that the absence of God must be irrelevant to it—just as the reality of God does not depend on the believer's morality, which is what any believer knows, and Ivan too. In short whether everything is permissible cannot proceed from the hypothesis of God's absence, regardless of how much Euclidian fanaticism one deploys in favor of the contrary argument.

And Ivan, we suspect, knows this, at least when he declares: "I must have justice, or I will destroy myself. And not justice in some remote infinite time and space, but here on earth, and that I could see myself. I have believed in it. I want to see it, and if I am dead by then, let me rise again, for if it all happens without me, it will be too unfair. Surely I haven't suffered, simply that I, my crimes and my sufferings, may manure the soil for the future harmony for somebody else. I want to see with my own eyes the hind lie down with the lion and the victim rise up and embrace his murderer. I want to be there when every one suddenly understands what it has all been for. All the religions of the world are built on this longing, and I am a believer."[9]

In the light of such a declaration what else can we observe, except that Ivan's refutation of God's existence is but the ultimate expression of doubt, the only kind of doubt that is not obliterated but can be assumed by faith alone, and that catapults the unbeliever into faith even while he says, "I do not believe till I see." As Dostoevski remarks, the believer is a realist whose doubt is strong enough to be assumed by his faith, like Alyosha, who, we are told, "was more of a realist than any one." To which Dostoevski adds: "Oh! no doubt, in the monastery he fully believed in miracles, but, to my thinking, miracles are never a stumbling-block to the realist. It is not miracles that dispose realists to belief. The genuine realist, if he is an unbeliever, will always find strength and ability to disbelieve in the miraculous, and if he is confronted with a miracle as an irrefutable fact he would rather disbelieve his own senses than admit the fact. Even if he admits it, he admits it as a fact of nature till then unrecognized by him. Faith does not, in the realist, spring from the miracle but the miracle from faith. If the realist once believes, then he is bound by his very realism to admit the miraculous also."[10]

In this light, it must also be noted that *The Brothers Karamazov* moves from one focus to the other, from

Ivan to Alyosha, while the ellipse corresponding to these foci is drawn by the rôle of Father Zossima, whose character stands like a framework to the novel.

Brilliant and highly educated, Ivan is a Euclidian intellect, for whom what the intellect cannot ultimately demonstrate, man cannot believe; and what is not ultimately rational as well as rationally ultimate need not be believed, anyway. Of the many definitions of reason, Ivan's is the furthest removed from Pascal's, who said that nothing so conformed with the reason as its own disavowal of itself. Ivan loves children, and is in love with Katherine Ivanovna, but he remains unable to acknowledge that life has any meaning. Unable to accept the world as it is, symbolically he hands back his ticket for admission into it. Nevertheless, it is not God whom he rejects, at least on the surface, so much as His purposeless creation, in which one thing intolerably obsesses him—the suffering of innocent children.[11]

What Ivan actually does is simply abstain from attacking the problem of God's existence, frontally. Being, as Alyosha points out to Rakitin, "one of those who don't want millions, but an answer to their questions,"[12] his first step is to leave the question of God aside, in order to establish the practicability of atheism. If he succeeds in this then he will have also shown in addition that, whether God exists or not, he is irrelevant to the problems of life and his reality has no bearing on the situation of man. Morality must be possible without immortality. But Ivan does not take into account that such a possibility, as we have suggested and as we learn while the focus moves from Ivan to Alyosha, is precisely what cannot logically nullify the question of God.

As for the paramount question, an answer to which Ivan prefers to millions, what can it be, if it is not the question of God? Ivan himself puts his finger on it, when he tells the legend of the Grand Inquisitor. We can easily guess it. What Ivan's Euclidian intellect attempts to formulate beyond dispute, and fails, is the question that will obliterate the question of God. He fails, perhaps because Dostoevski seems to suggest, this would amount to obliterating the question of man itself. Indeed, almost like Smerdyakov, who finally disbelieves his own disbelief when he commits suicide, Ivan seems to realize the insuperable obstacles confronting rationalism and the dilemma over which rationalism agonizes: should reason lead to some kind of immanentist deism, it would immediately cease to be reasonable; should rationalism set up a religion of reason, it would contradict itself.

Both furthest away from Ivan and closest to him is Alyosha. In particular, he too is a Karamazov, Dostoevski most emphatically points out. Through him, the entire Karamazov family is redeemed in the end. Not because he withdraws into a monastery, away from the world and its miseries; not because he wants to flee from life; but because, as Father Zossima enjoins him to do, he assumes, as he must, the task of existence by assuming the reality of the world, where contradiction succeeds to harmony, and destiny is usurped but not overcome by the defeats of existence. No more than Ivan can he tolerate the suffering of innocent children, but he does not claim to know enough to blame it on God or on His creation. And, whereas Ivan seeks the security of a system, Alyosha casts his lot with the downtrodden and the rejected, with those who suffer innocently. He is not self-righteous, whether before God or, like Ivan, before himself. He truly incarnates Zossima's faith, so that to both of them can be applied Luther's definition of the Christian: "a Christian man is the most free lord of all, subject to none; a Christian man is the most dutiful servant of all, subject to everyone."

Father Zossima is, moreover, the answer to the Grand Inquisitor. A former army man whose family were landowners, he has become the honor and glory of the monastery. But he has not quitted life, or departed from the living. By withdrawing into the seclusion of the monastery, he has neither abdicated nor escaped from the responsibilities of life. In contrast to those who seek to prove their heroism in life he brings into light the fact that life must be accepted in the totality of its moments of joy and sorrow. And, in particular, he shows that life is not a ready-made answer to some abstract question far removed from reality, but a question mark in the very moment of each decision. Lying sick in his cell, he is venerated by the multitudes who expect his death to be miraculous, and who thereby prove how little they understand his asceticism, let alone his faith. He dies, and rots, the way all mortals do, but confronting his survivors with a truth they would rather evade: those who seek miracles can be as atheistic as those who rebel against the suffering of the innocent and hope for some miraculous system that would correct the creation. Religiosity is a plague whether it drapes itself into the mantle of faith or with that of atheism. In neither case does it face the question of God, but seeks to avoid it. And that is what the legend of the Grand Inquisitor also teaches us.

A proper understanding of the legend necessitates that we begin with the discussion between Ivan and Alyosha that takes place in the preceding chapter, and deals with the suffering of innocent children. That innocent children suffer only proves to Ivan that "the world stands on absurdities, and perhaps nothing would have come to pass in it without them. We know what we know." And, he adds, "all I know is that there is suffering and that there are none guilty."[13] Therefore, Ivan concludes, there is no justice. And even if justice were done here and now, how could a mother forgive "the suffering of her tortured child"? How could there be "in the whole world a being who would have the right to forgive and could forgive,"[14] even if Ivan himself were wrong, as he also carefully admits?

There are two edges to his argument. The first one, contrary to the intention of his logic, actually cuts the ground from under it: indeed, if there were any justice, would we not all be guilty? We would, and that is why we suspect that Ivan is not so much concerned about justice as about self-justification. For the same reason, his desperate groping for something to believe beyond dispute would finally lead him not to justice here on earth but to a blind legal system, consistency with which would demand from him that he take the law into his own hands, that he revenge himself, or that he commit suicide. Thus, either we would all be judges—and, indeed, are we not, since "there are none guilty"? Or suicide would be the only valid act that would exonerate us from the freedom by which everything is permissible and lawful.

The second edge is the one with which Ivan attempts to cut God off from the pursuit of morality. God is irrelevant to the moral problem, such would be Ivan's allegation as we stated earlier; but he adds a new twist to it—the legend of the Grand Inquisitor: has not religion itself (which, Ivan acknowledges, has a similar quest for justice in common with his own dream) made God irrelevant to the moral problem? Is it not true, he convincingly questions us in his relentless legend, that this side of immortality men prefer bread to freedom, that they compromise their freedom for the sake of bread, and that the Inquisitor (i.e., religion) sanctions this compromise allegedly in the name of some loftier obedience to God, whereas this compromise is exactly what flouts justice here on earth? And does it not follow then that religion, too, is some form of practical atheism —not unlike his own?

As Eduard Thurneysen has judiciously remarked in

his penetrating study,[15] what Ivan has brought into evidence through the legend of the Grand Inquisitor is that religion is based on a lie, and what he has aimed at is a compelling demonstration of atheism as religion and of religion as practical atheism. But we must add that Ivan's purpose is not merely to point out the sinful alliances of religion; it is to show that atheism, too, can be quite practical, indeed as practical as religion. Atheism, as Ivan perspicaciously makes clear, need not be metaphysical. In fact, the less metaphysical it is the more practical and consistent with itself it will be. Who, indeed, is more concerned about practical things than the Grand Inquisitor himself? Only, Ivan insinuates, one no longer needs religion to be an atheist, though there may still linger a certain kinship between religion and unbelief: the Devil himself confesses to Ivan later on in the novel that he finds himself completely at ease in churches. Furthermore, by laying bare the atheism of religion, the "iconoclastic" Ivan also lays bare the idolatrousness into which the Christian tradition atrophies whenever it ceases to be iconoclastic. It takes iconoclastic audacity to believe in God, and God cleaves man from himself as much as he makes him whole again.

Neither Ivan nor the Grand Inquisitor, neither metaphysical nor practical atheism, takes into account that faith in God is something more than a social philosophy. Not that it must be dissociated from social realities. But it cannot be measured only from the standpoint of a

socio-economical reductionism. God is not to be identified with social progress, or with happiness written
large and idealized. Since faith in God is always somewhat utopian, it cannot conform with this or that ecclesiastic organization any more than it can conform
with this or that ideal, social, economic, or political. The
more authentic and the more iconoclastic faith is, the
more it disavows the ideals that man, in his weakness,
identifies it by. As worthy a cause as the amelioration
of man's condition can be, it is bound to fail or to lead
to delusion if it loses sight of the essential element,
namely Christ—to speak Dostoevski's language—or the
fact that man's being is essentially utopian, that man's
happiness does not lie here or there, in this or that
social, economic, political solution, even though there
is no happiness without this world, here and now.

"The West has become Christ-less," wrote Dostoevski,
"through the fault of Catholicism . . . and the West is
declining because of that, and only because of that."[16]
It is not the atheists who are responsible for the death
of God, but Christianity itself. Christendom has made
it possible, by substituting the accommodating com-
placencies of religiosity for the exigent demands that
accompany the act of faith in a transcendent God. Indeed, the iconoclastic quality of faith can be recognized
by this: it does not seek to bring God's transcendent
reality down to the level of finite and immanent realities
in order to fuse them. Moreover, the utopian nature of
man's being implies that man is at home both every-

where and nowhere; between his finitude and God's infinity there is such a radical difference that man, as a transcendental being, cannot overcome it by satisfying himself either with any kind of reductionism that would progressively invalidate the notion of God, or with his own self-deification. Those who proclaim that God is *de trop* are just as much the victims of immanentist religiosity as the Grand Inquisitor.

Indeed, if by religiosity is meant any system that in the long run makes God superfluous, the Grand Inquisitor is the apostle par excellence of religiosity. What he offers his flock is exactly what Ivan is longing for—something to be believed beyond dispute, in terms of which man's being would not be governed by transcendental aspirations. Like Ivan's atheism, the Inquisitor's religiosity denies God by denying at once the iconoclastic and the utopian qualities of faith. Ivan knows of this complicity with the Inquistor, but what he does not yet fully realize is that the denial of God is but another form of immanentist religiosity. Meanwhile, it becomes evident that one cannot prevent the spoliation of man by any Grand Inquisitor, and that Ivan's ideal cannot be applied, unless every man were to become his fellowman's inquisitor: *Homo homini deus*. As Berdyaev has pointed out, the road which leads to the deification of man is that which generally results in the system of Shigaliev and of the Grand Inquisitor.[17]

God is dead as soon as faith ceases to be eschatological, that is, at once iconoclastic and utopian, and turns into a turgid religiosity, carefully cloistered by the walls of its compromises with the world, like an ostrich burying its head in the sand. Then faith gives way to the religiosity of bread and circuses, of the social question, of the Kingdom of God on earth. But when faith is truly eschatological, then the Kingdom of God is viewed not as the secularization of some otherworldly bliss, but as the "desecularization" of this world. Much has been said against the religiosity of pie-in-the-sky, and justifiably so. Very little emphasis, however, has been put on the necessity of exposing the compensating idolatrous approach to the world, on the need to desecularize this world. In the legend of the Grand Inquisitor, Dostoevski's criticism is directed as much against the depraved religiosity of otherworldliness as against the surreptitious idolization of this world. For their common denominator is the conscious or unconscious proclamation that God is dead, the conscious or unconscious deification of man for which all pretexts are good, from rebellion against the suffering of the innocent to the Euclidian self-satisfaction derived from a geometric conception of justice—the kind of justice which is as clear-cut as a guillotine.

This aspect of the legend is best grasped from the standpoint of the antinomy between freedom and happiness, in the light of which, to begin with, Ivan presents his indictment of Christianity.

Because freedom has degenerated into happiness, the legend does not imply that they are incompatible. When

Walter Kaufmann contends that they are irreconcilable, he imputes to Dostoevski's understanding of freedom an otherworldly quality, and points out that happiness is a this-worldly goal.[18] But this apparent reliance on the classical antinomy between this world and the next does not exonerate Kaufmann from arbitrarily removing Dostoevski's understanding of freedom from the context of the biblical tradition that informs it. Nor must we forget that Dostoevski's concern about social justice is dependent upon the question of God. For this reason, we venture the suggestion that even the antinomy between freedom and happiness does not make sense, unless we take into account Dostoevski's implicit definition of real freedom. For it is clear that by freedom he does not mean that which people abdicate for the sake of bread. He means the freedom of the Christian, of the new man in Christ, of the new being, as exemplified by Father Zossima and lived by Alyosha, here and now, in the world. Correspondingly, it is also evident that by happiness Dostoevski refers to inauthentic existence. And what existence could be more inauthentic than that of those who for the sake of religious security have abdicated their birthright, abdicated that which was given them by grace?

In other terms, the antinomy between freedom and happiness is similar to that between faith and good works. Without good works, faith is dead. But good works are no substitute for faith. Without happiness, freedom is irrelevant to man's situation in this world.

Without freedom, social institutions are dead or deadly. The freedom that is derived from grace transcends all institutions, be they social or ecclesiastical. And it is the exercise of this freedom that results in the creation of institutions. Institutions do not create freedom; they can only create its substitute: "A free people," observed Montesquieu, "is not that which is determined by such and such form of government; it is that which enjoys the form of government established by law."[19] Just as faith may not claim to take refuge in any safe institutional religion, so also freedom is not guaranteed by any political institution. Freedom can sink into its caricature, cheap happiness, even as faith can sink into religiosity. Is this not what Alyosha means, when he promptly points up to Ivan that the legend is, indeed, in praise of Christ?

But people will always settle for any soteriological system as they will settle for any social, economic, and political one, out of subservience to a feared authoritarian regime or to the equally feared authoritarianism of conformity. People will always forget that faith, or authentic freedom, is an eschatological reality, from the standpoint of which existence is no logical consistency, but a succession of coherent as well as incoherent facts. In other words, happiness is to freedom as rationalized belief is to faith, or as logical consistency is to eschatological existence—as Ivan is to Alyosha. And the dilemma between freedom and happiness is but another aspect of the dilemma between faith as eschatological existence, or as radical commitment, of the type of Father Zossima's, on the one hand, and "peace of mind," on the other, the poor man's impoverished version of Ivan's rebellion against evil, of Ivan's quest for the miraculous answer to his questions.

Could it be that Ivan too has rejected freedom for the sake of some indisputable demonstration? He puts these words in the mouth of the Grand Inquisitor: "Instead of taking man's freedom from them, Thou didst make it greater than ever! Didst Thou forget that man prefers peace, and even death to freedom of choice in the knowledge of good and evil?"[20] And does not Ivan's rationalism seek to prove something, even while he knows that faith proves nothing, not even the existence of God? "Thou didst hope that man, following Thee, would cling to God and not ask for a miracle. But Thou didst not know that when man rejects miracle he rejects God too; for man seeks not so much God as the miraculous."[21] Yes, Ivan himself seeks the miraculous; consider the tortured question he throws at the Devil, later on: "Is there a God or not?" Even by his own definition of freedom, Ivan knows that "so long as man remains free he strives for nothing so incessantly and so painfully as to find someone to worship."[22]

But Ivan also knows his own weakness; he knows that the weakness of arrogant defiance against God is precisely the same as that of the submissive religiosity of the flock over which the Inquisitor rules. Indeed, at this point, the Inquisitor is really Ivan's spokesman, especially when he rebukes Jesus by saying: "Choosing bread, Thou wouldst have satisfied the universal and everlasting craving of humanity—to find some one to worship . . . to worship what is established beyond dispute."[23] Clearly, bread or religiosity and logical consistency or the Euclidian intellect are interchangeable terms. On the one hand, when religion is based on bread, it is merely seeking something to worship beyond dispute—as atheism itself is doing, and as is demonstrated by Ivan's intellectual, rationalistic quest for logical consistency. On the other hand, when reason is simply identified with logical consistency, it is no less seeking something that might be established beyond dispute— and believed.

And yet what do these self-righteous or tortured gropings mean? What are they but signs—maimed by complacency yet eloquently outraged—still signs of man's quest for God? Significantly, the Grand Inquisitor, abject as he is, is kissed by his Prisoner. Alyosha kisses Ivan. Alyosha knows that the "God in whom (Ivan) disbelieved, and His truth were gaining mastery over his heart, which still refused to submit."[24]

One must view the work of Dostoevski as an attempt to retrace the transcendental values gradually eliminated since the advent of the modern period. To be sure, he is also aware that certain changes have meanwhile taken place, and they cannot be denied. But he rebels against the desecration of man that has resulted from them. For him man is a spiritual being and though his characters remain human to the fullest extent, men of flesh and bones, what matters is the spirit that animates them.

Ultimately what Dostoevski has been concerned with is the problem of faith in God in an age that renders it hardly practical, in which both culture and religiosity militate against it. Like Tolstoy, Dostoevski endeavored, as Thurneysen observes, to reconcile man with his conscience and his culture.[25] Indeed, in some way culture represents man's bad conscience. No one can participate in culture without dirty hands, as the legend of the Grand Inquisitor shows with great power. Nor can one accomplish one's task as a man without dirty hands. On this point, Dostoevski and Tolstoy part company, for the latter sought in vain to be a man and not dirty his hands —almost like Ivan and unlike Alyosha.

PÄR LAGERKVIST:
Hell Is God

****

IT NEED not be the wrath of God that points to the ineluctable difference between God and man. It may be the love of God. To see God and live, that is to say, to be sure of one's faith, may be relatively easy, when God is first reduced to the convenient attributes of a blind idol. It is incomparably more difficult to be sure of one's sight, or for that matter, of one's hearing and, by the same token, of one's faith when the transcendence of God confronts man through the debility and transitoriness of an historical event set, as it always seems to be, among other similarly ordinary events. For no event is in itself a proof of God's reality, although every event reveals God as much as it conceals him. Faith, in other words, presupposes God's hiddenness as much as his

193

revelation. That is why, according to the Old Testament, in faith no one can see God and live; and in this condition can be recognized the believer's paradoxical assurance that nothing will separate him from the love of God.

Lagerkvist's novel, *Barabbas*, is the story of a man who continually seeks and rejects this kind of faith or trust in the love of God. It is the story of a man whom nothing can separate from God's presence—not even God's absence. From the wandering Jew to the dispossessed Chirstian, it is the story of every man, who either has no place to come from or, like Mary Magdalene, has no place to stand on because, as she exclaimed when she saw the empty tomb, "they have taken my Lord away."

For that reason, the novel begins on Good Friday and ends on another Good Friday, when the protagonist himself is also crucified. It begins with the so-called redemptive answer to man's predicament (on Jesus' Good Friday) and ends with the question raised by this predicament itself (on Barabbas' Good Friday). Do they have anything in common? They are, it seems, as different as man is from God. Neither Good Friday has anything in common with the other, except gratuitousness, perhaps. And that, precisely, is what—like grace itself—cannot be measured, just as a miracle proves only that it proves nothing.

In this novel, there is nothing extraordinary about Barabbas' Good Friday. For his part in spreading the fire of Rome, he is crucified together with a good many

Christians whose expectation of the Parousia (that is, of Christ's return) made its hoped-for imminence symbolic of their ineradicable faith. But, the crucifixion of Barabbas is that of a lonely man, a derelict. It serves only to stress the contradictions and confusion of his life. And, more significantly, it stands for the average Good Friday of an average man, for whom God's absence is as inexorable as his presence. It solves no problems, but raises new questions.

What this means is that the inescapable failure of human destiny in its very final unfolding is not final, ultimate. It is "unfinished," just as much as man's inescapable birth. What man leaves behind is always something unfinished. And because the contradictions of existence, too, are unfinished, they are not final either. Nor are the answers men usually give to the dilemma that confronts human existence from birth to death. Despair itself can never be, accordingly, indicative of the ultimate reality of life, and does not give the clue to its meaning. In human terms, real despair is ultimately (if tragically) such that it must consent to despair of itself, and thus overcome the anguish that contradicts man's hope and makes it superfluous. So that, mutilated as hope always is, it remains valid and authentic as a sign that man's journey has a destiny.

Lagerkvist himself asks: "Are we the happier because we seek the truth? I know not. I merely seek it. All my life has been a restless search for it, and sometimes I have felt that I have apprehended it, I have caught a glimpse of its pure sky—but the sky has never opened itself to me, my eyes have never filled themselves with its endless spaces, without which nothing here can be fully understood. It is not vouchsafed to us. Therefore all I have touched has been but partly true and partly completed. I think of my works with pain and so they will be regarded by all—as though they were a torso. All that I have created is imperfect and unfinished. All that I leave behind is unfinished.

"But is there anything strange in that? It is the fate of mankind, the inescapable destiny of all human effort and all human achievement. Is it ever more than an attempt, an attempt at something which is not meant to be achieved by any of us? All human culture is but an attempt at something unattainable, something which far transcends our powers of realization. There it stands, mutilated, tragic as a torso. Is not the human spirit itself a torso?"[1]

Although his settings and characters are frequently sketched in terms of light and darkness, it seems wrong to attribute to Lagerkvist a dualistic apprehension of the world and of life. Life can be sorted out neither in terms of light and darkness nor in terms of good and evil. Nor can we assume that Lagerkvist's analysis leans toward a monistic understanding of reality. Even if there is no self-evident demarcation line between good and evil, the novelist is not contending that good and evil are the same thing. The darkness that pervades so many of Lagerkvist's novels is, thus, always dark enough to let the reader catch a glimpse of the light on the other side of human existence. And, in spite of the tragedy, Lagerkvist's analysis of man's condition always reveals a translucent facet, even in the darkest dereliction.

In the last resort, the meaning of existence is not maimed by darkness, nor even by man's helplessness. Nor is it withered by despair. Above and beyond the cries of anguish, love remains a possibility, and hope is susceptible of incarnation even if incredibly. Love and love only, because it is not more and not less than a possibility, can expose the artifacts of doubt and show at once its ultimate nakedness and its readiness for faith. Only love can rebel against its own injustice, and therefore go out of itself to meet the anguish of others. Love is the key that unlocks this anguish and deciphers existence. "Love is something which dies and when dead it rots and becomes soil for a new love." And yet the final meaning of Lagerkvist's work is equivocal.

It is ambivalent. For example, Lagerkvist hardly gives his readers any clue to his characters. He lets us guess. But the guess itself takes the form of a question. Meaning is dichotomous, and Lagerkvist's work yields no meaning in terms of light and darkness, sacred and secular, etc.; but it does yield a question. In fact, the meaning of his work seems to be centered around a question that is itself projected into an unceasing quest. And life thus discloses its meaningfulness despite (or through) its meaninglessness.

Brought up as a Lutheran, Lagerkvist recently called

himself a "religious atheist." A novelist, poet, and play-wright, he received the Nobel prize in 1951. Outside his native Sweden he is generally known for *The Dwarf* (dealing with the hypocrisy of Renaissance man), *The Eternal Smile* (a collection of short stories), and *The Death of Ahasuerus,* the recent publication of which in English was preceded by *Barabbas* and *The Sibyl.* Here we are concerned especially with the last two books.

Barabbas[3] is a tightly written novel about the man who, according to the gospels, was released instead of Jesus. The fact that the name means "son of the master" and that Barabbas himself is referred to by some manu-scripts known to Origen as Jesus Barabbas is not with-out importance. Was Barabbas possibly one of those who claimed to be the Messiah? We must note that this claim is not wholly glossed over in the novel. When Barabbas insinuates now and then that he would have acted differently from Jesus, not only do we wonder what a messiah is; we realize how precarious the basis of Jesus' messiahship is. And by what, anyway, shall we know a messiah? By his fruits? Let us, then, delve into the novel itself.

It was suggested earlier that Barabbas represented every man. More especially, he represents every Chris-tian on behalf of whom Jesus is crucified. But let us take a closer look. This man, as depicted by Lagerkvist, rep-resents every man only by virtue of those incredible niceties that religiosity fosters in the heart of the hypo-crite, in the easy conscience of Christianity. In reality

I am not Barabbas; I am not the real Barabbas. It is easy to be a Christian, as is shown by one Christian after another with whom Barabbas comes into contact. It is more difficult to be Barabbas and, particularly, one who wants to become a Christian. By thus intimating to the Christian that he really does not know what it means to be Barabbas, Lagerkvist is not attempting merely a smart criticism of Christianity. His purpose is more serious than that. It is to show—and he does this successfully— that existence itself is hypocritical. And religiosity in particular is the hypocrisy by which existence fails. Barabbas is thus the story of man in search of God as well as of a self. Such a man is one who can never be the same again, whether because, like Barabbas, he has "seen" Jesus being crucified in his stead; or because man has been, so to speak, once visited by God and he can never forget it, even if nothing more than a shattered image of this encounter lingers in his memory. Lagerkvist's succinct portrayal applies to either type of man.

When the novel begins, it is Good Friday. Barabbas is watching the crucifixion from his hiding place. He gazes at the cross, at that incredible messiah. He gazes at the crowd, and again at that incredible messiah, who suddenly cries, "My God, my God, why hast thou forsaken me?" Already, Barabbas is no longer the murderer: never is he to be the same again. Neither when, back in town, he seeks out his people; nor when he makes love because there is nothing else to do. But sex is no substitute for the darkness of Golgotha and its obsession. The crucifixion haunts him.

Barabbas tries to be himself. He seeks out the company of Christians in the slums of Jerusalem. They reject him, not without evincing some kind of pharisaic and supernaturalistic attachment to Jesus. Only two of that group stand out: a harelipped woman and Peter. The woman's sole desire is to witness the resurrection with Barabbas. Later on, she is condemned and stoned: the first stone must be cast by her accuser—a blind man, who keeps missing her, thus symbolizing the aimlessness of self-righteousness. Barabbas himself, who has been watching this execution too, wants to do something but it is not said whether for the sake of the woman, or her God, or out of sheer revulsion. The other character, Peter, resembles Barabbas at least physically. They have similar beards. Both have striking eyes. But Barabbas' are empty. And Peter's denials prefigure those of Barabbas in the second part of the novel.

That part takes the reader to the Cyprian copper mines, where Barabbas serves out a sentence of hard labor. The convicts are chained in pairs. Barabbas' companion is a Christian, Sahak, who embodies the ideal of brotherly love. Freed for his exemplarity, he refuses to be separated from Barabbas in the name of Jesus whose symbol is engraved on a disk hanging from a chain he is wearing around his neck. Barabbas, too, by that time wears one. Finally, because of his unflinching witness to Jesus Christ, Sahak is crucified. Barabbas, by contrast, is spared again. But then the reader notices that the Christ symbol on his disk has been crossed out.

At the end of the novel the action takes place in Rome. Again, Barabbas seeks out the small group of Christians. One night, he suddenly realizes that he is spreading the fire that is burning Rome and that will be blamed on the Christians. Why? Is he on the madman's side and attempting to harm the Christian community? Or is he hoping against hope to hasten the end of it all? Barabbas is caught, still wearing that chain and that disk with the crossed-out symbol; somehow he has not thrown it away. Even so, he is rejected, once again, by those Christians with whom he is imprisoned and awaits to be crucified.

"And so they were crucified. They were chained together in pairs, and, as they were not an even number, Barabbas came last in the procession, not chained to anyone. It just turned out like that.

". . . The crucified spoke consolingly and hopefully to each other the whole time. To Barabbas nobody spoke.

"When dusk fell the spectators had already gone. . . . The crucified were all dead.

"Only Barabbas was left hanging there alone, still alive. When he felt death approaching, that which he had always been so afraid of, he said out into the darkness, as though he were speaking to it:

" 'To thee I deliver up my soul.'
"And he gave up the ghost." [4]

As André Gide has remarked, everything hangs on that "as though."[5] It was said earlier that Barabbas' eyes were empty. But were they not always, as now they are, at his death, filled with darkness, the ultimate night of the soul in which despair prefigures the irruption of God's inexorable presence; in which suffering is accepted as a gift of God, as a token of God's bottomless and formidable presence from which there is no fleeing?[6]

Barabbas thus accepts his own suffering. The only thing he cannot accept is the suffering of others, just as he cannot accept the suffering and the evil caused by man. Now we can at last spell out the question that haunted Barabbas: by what right does man jump from the contradictions of existence and the impossibility of ironing them out to the allegation that they contradict the existence of God?

Clearly, then, the problem of God is the problem of man, even if by the end of the novel, God seems to be utterly indifferent to man—or utterly different from man. Whether present or absent, God is incomprehensible except to him who is found by God, and who has faith and believes that God can and does comprehend man. Faith means being understood and reintegrated, even if one's existence is blurred or erased as is the symbol of God's presence on Barabbas' disk. Surely, faith "confers no secure knowledge," as Karl Jaspers states in *Way to Wisdom*.[7] And that is why existence is so incomplete and its incompletion of such a quality that no secure knowledge can ever give it completion. Those who have this faith, writes Lagerkvist, "seem happy, whether from simple-mindedness or some other cause—perhaps because of their faith; that is what they say themselves of course. And it may be true."[8]

The Sibyl is the story of God's love, his cruel love, which strikes like lightning. It is the story of every man, told about a man whose eyes have the look of eyes that have seen God. In contrast to *Barabbas*, the theme of *The Sibyl* intertwines and synchronizes both Christianity and the Delphic cult of Apollo.

As the novel opens, a man standing at the door of his house in the town where he was born sees a stranger dragging himself with his cross. Nothing unusual about this. The man with the cross wants to lean against the house for a brief pause. Being told to move on, he curses the house-owner who, accordingly, shall never find rest, not even that of death. He is Jesus.

After an agonizing interval, the house-owner sets out on his spiritual journey, and wanders until he finds the Sibyl (a woman reputed to have powers of prophecy and divination), in order to ask her what the future holds for him. But the Sibyl herself is the object of a curse, also. By the time the wanderer meets her, the following events have already taken place.

Carefully set apart from the other girls of her town, she had been consecrated to be Apollo's Pythia at the Temple of Delphi. As such she became, so to speak, God's bride. All is well in the beginning, and in her humility she is thankful to God for her having been chosen to fulfill his purpose. It is as if she had been called out, set apart by God himself—not unlike the Virgin Mary.

Then she falls in love, and becomes pregnant. But her adultery is more than a profanation of her religious calling. While it does bring about her material misfortune, it also seems to apply to God himself the malediction that, according to the Old Testament, God reserves for those who do not keep his commandment: "You shall betroth a wife and another man shall lie with her." And, besides, God seems to have connived with the priests of the Temple, and shared in their greed and dishonesty. The priests and everyone else had led the Pythia to believe that her vocation was a special mark of God's grace, whereas, she had actually been chosen simply because the job was an exhausting one and the more sophisticated and well-to-do females of the town by far preferred the less rigorous demands of a real man's sexual favors.

When the Sibyl discovers the duplicity, her faith crumbles, the hypocritical religion of the Temple loses its mask, and God topples. The pious, motherly woman who looked after her material welfare was in fact spying on her behavior, watching for symptoms of pregnancy, by which the Pythia would be disqualified. Except for the janitor, the whole Temple turns against the Sibyl. Meanwhile, her lover drowns in the river, a twig in his hand: accident or suicide, the fact remains uncertain, save for the twig, which symbolizes God's signature. But the comfort and consolation of God are of no more help than a twig that a drowning man may grasp in his desperation.

The Sibyl finally succeeds in escaping to the mountains; there, she gives birth to her child. Reflecting on the length of her pregnancy, she calculates that the child must have been conceived on a day when she was performing her pythiac functions. Had therefore the child been conceived by God?

The child is an idiot.

The parallelism between Mary and the Sibyl continues until the child one day disappears in the mountains.

But the heart of the story is concerned with the encounter between God and man. Some people say that such an encounter is possible, and, at least for those who believe it, this may be true. But how could one tell whether the child was God's child, or whether the encounter was with God? Cleaving to man, this dilemma becomes a source of joy and suffering, of anguish and peace; a blessing and a curse, it becomes the source of an invincible doubt and a labyrinthine faith. "God is merciless . . . like lightning. Suddenly it strikes, suddenly he strikes down on one, revealing all his cruelty. Or his love—his cruel love."[9]

But surely the wandering man had set out on his quest to find or to be told more than just this. Or else his quest would be as meaningless in the end as it was in the

beginning. Is existence as destitute as the wandering
man's eyes are empty, "depths with nothing in them"?
The Sibyl saw that "it was not so. They were not empty.
They were full of despair."[10] And despair comes from
the desire to look into the future and realizing that
there is no place where God stands closer to man than
when man stands furthest from him. Is this not what the
Sibyl means when she says to the wanderer: "I can see
in your face that you're under God's curse and that what
you say is true. It's plain that you're not free, that
you're bound to him and that he doesn't mean to let you
go. He is your destiny. Your soul is filled with him;
through his curse you live a life with God. You hate
him, you mock and revile him. But judging by your in-
dignant words you care for nothing in the world but
him, and are filled with him alone. . . .

"You want me to look into the future. . . . [Man's]
destiny will always be bound up with God." [11]

In *Barabbas*, Lagerkvist presents the image of a man
for whom destiny seems always too late. In *The Sibyl*,
destiny always waits for man.

FRANZ KAFKA:
The Atheist's Problem of God

✳✳✳✳✳✳✳✳✳✳✳✳✳✳✳✳✳✳✳✳✳✳✳✳✳

KAFKA the lucid could not help it if his morbidity
was to become an instrument of frustrated catharsis for
our generation; nor could he prevent his logic from
enshrining the absurd in the breast of modern man.
Neither a totalitarian nor a moralist, he denounced the
morality of dogmatism as well as the dogmatism of religion. And when in his work he passes over God in
silence, he forces us to realize that God is no longer the
missing link we boast of in justifying ourselves or our
loud religiosities.

Not a prophet, nor claiming to be one, it is not
Kafka's fault if we find in his work, in the illusory
world of his tales and parables, the mirror that reflects
the upside-down image of our present condition.

He received no mandate ever from anyone, did not even speak in his own name. Simply seeking to grasp the illusion of a reality—his own—that cannot comprehend itself, he now confronts us with the reality of our own illusion—with no other reality than that of our illusions about God, about man, about the world, justice, and humanity.

Coming from the very heart of man's night, Kafka's voice immediately dispels the deafness into which we have complacently sunk our hearing. But what we hear is not what he said. What we understand is not what he meant. Yet he did say it and he did mean it. But each of us can grasp and understand it only in his own way. We could apply to him his parable of the Sirens: "These are the seductive voices of the night; the Sirens, too, sang that way. It would be doing them an injustice to think that they wanted to seduce; they knew they had claws and sterile wombs, and they lamented this aloud. They could not help it if their laments sounded so beautiful." [1]

And what was it Kafka lamented so loudly and so beautifully? It was the possibility of our being many selves at once or alternately, of being more than oneself and by the same token less than oneself; in other words, it was the impossibility of being oneself, of taking up residence in oneself or, to recall Saint Augustine, of resting in oneself. But I am preaching. Kafka himself was no preacher: he did not embellish and try to improve upon his master's teachings. By the time of

Kafka, anyway, no teaching was left that could sustain improvement. Is that not why he did not talk about God —or, for that matter, about man? He merely describes the situation of man, the logic of its incoherence as well as the contradictions of its logic.

What is man? A *flatus vocis*, a name reduced to its anonymous initial, a word that does not become flesh. "I lack nothing," observes Kafka, "except myself." He who so much loved precision, Max Brod tells us in his biography,[2] never cared fully to explain his characters. He believed in a world of exactness, in the indestructible, and yet uncertainty rules over his universe; man is frustrated from attaining the fullness of his being. He is nameless, because God is dead.

Or is it so? For we must remember that Kafka does not preach, either for or against God. He does not say that this is what man is like without God, namely wretched and desperate. Nor does he say that the idea of God is absurd. What, then, is he saying? Perhaps, that it is man's wretchedness itself that is absurd, because it prevents us from knowing our real condition as well as the real world unfailingly, although it exists. As Max Brod writes, "truth is visible everywhere. It shines through the nets of what we call 'reality.' "[3]

Man has been secularized. He has been thoroughly *laïcisé*. In 1914, Kafka enters in his diary this reflection: "What do I have in common with the Jews? I have hardly anything in common with myself, and I should keep quiet in a corner, content that I can breathe."

Having nothing in common with himself, man has nothing in common with God, either. Of course, Kafka does not say that, since he never mentions God in his stories. With or without God, man is that being which has nothing in common with itself. Even less does he have anything in common with God. And it is hard to say which comes first, the absence of God or man's absence from himself.

Or are we digressing from Kafka by reading between the lines? Indeed, it might be objected, is not Kafka simply proclaiming the death of God? The answer is twofold. We must admit, to be sure, that Kafka is recording the cultural dimension of that event. As to whether, on the other hand, he also proclaims such an event, we may not answer this question affirmatively before we have realized, as Jean Starobinski points out in his introduction to *La Colonie pénitentiaire*, that this blasphemy—if blasphemy there is—is also a prayer, an invocation.[4] Admittedly, like all logic, the logic of blasphemy, too, imposes itself. It is self-evident and ineluctable, like a trial verdict that has been handed down beforehand. But, unshakable as logic can be, it breaks down before the will to live (cf. Jean Wahl, *Esquisse pour une histoire de l'existentialisme*):

"No one can say that we are wanting in faith. The mere fact of our living is itself inexhaustible in its proof of faith.

"You call that a proof of faith? But one simply cannot live.

"In that very 'simply cannot' lies the insane power of faith; in that denial it embodies itself." [5]

What kind of denial, of negation are we dealing with here? Clearly, we are first of all dealing with the negation into which life incarnates itself. As Camus would say: "I rebel, therefore we are." Kafka's man is a man who says no; more precisely, he ends up saying no simply because he has been saying nothing all along. But he cannot quite live on the logic of this no. Existence does not merely resolve itself into logical consistency. Thus, Kafka, who does not fully give us the key that would help us decipher his characters, hardly finishes his stories even when they are complete. He heralds the world of Picasso's *Guernica* as well as the advent of radical immanentism. He shows, too, that man cannot dwell in a universe of radical immanentism.

Kafka's particular merit is to have succeeded in translating into immanentist terms the values of a transcendental universe now discredited. Like Camus, he realized that the human spirit could conceive of the universe only from two possible angles—namely, that of the sacred (or that of grace) and that of rebellion.[6] These two are for both authors mutually exclusive. But unlike Camus, Kafka would also add that the universe of rebellion is (if one may say so) self-exclusive or self-negating; that is to say, it is one in which man lacks nothing but himself even when, as in *The Judgment*, all that is exhibited is not the irrationality of the Father's sentence, of God's justice, but the self-righteousness of Georg Bendemann and the senility of his father.

Kafka is not so much writing allegorical stories in which one thing consistently stands for another—for example the castle for God's grace—as he is writing about grace in immanentist terms, the only terms now meaningfully available. Perhaps this was a risky shot, an impossible bet. It can hardly be alleged that Kafka was a religious writer in the traditional sense, although he did consider the task of existing to be an act of faith, an invocation, a prayer, the only one that can be uttered when God is dead, that is, when God, ceasing to be a cultural accessory of man's self-understanding, can no longer be taken for granted.

Nor is Kafka writing symbolic novels in the traditional sense. He does not postulate the meaningfulness of a universe bearing out God's design for his creation and for man. To be sure, once God is thus posited as the universal hypothesis, it is easy to find symbols that point to his reality. But this kind of symbolism makes sense only in the context of a transcendental *Weltanschauung*, or, better, in the context of a sacramental universe in which nature points to a supernatural world. But, Kafka's world is one that has lost its sacral dimension. It does not presuppose any reality from which it receives its meaning and to which it points. As the French critic Jean Paulhan has remarked apropos of modern painting, Kafka's world is replete with signs and symbols crying out for that which they signify and that which they symbolize. Unfortunately, the power of the symbol does not come from its own capacity to point to that which is symbolized but lies in its capacity to receive, like a receptacle, and to communicate or mediate that which is symbolized. From the traditional point of view, the power of the symbol lies just in this charismatic instrumentality—in that through it, so to speak, the word becomes flesh.

Clearly, Kafka understood that it was no longer so for modern man. Modern man has the symbol but not the meaning. "We are digging the pit of Babel,"[7] as he put it. Or, "if it had been possible to build the tower of Babel without ascending it, the work would have been permitted."[8] This impotence of the symbol is further stressed in *The Great Wall of China,* where the riddle of existence takes the form of the problem: how to build a round tower on the foundations of a wall that is not circular? And whatever else the following "reflection" means, we can sense that, quite appropriately, it clarifies the analysis that concerns us here: "What is laid upon us is to accomplish the negative; the positive is already given."[9] Man has the words, but not the Word. In contrast with Sartre, Kafka says: "There is a goal, but no way; what we call the way is only wavering."[10]

Not that self-deification is the task of man, as is the case with Sartre; but the Word cannot be extracted from the words of man; it can only take flesh in them in the same way that God "dwells" in the Ark of the Covenant, and that happens through no merit either of the words or of the Ark, for their efficacy is charismatic. Perhaps this explains why Kafka's world looks so much like yours and mine, and is at the same time so fantastically different. We tend to act like positivists, he does not. No wonder, then, that the doorkeeper's words in the fragment "Before the Law," included also in *The Trial*, seem to address each of us: "No one else could ever be admitted here, since this gate was made only for you. I am now going to shut it."[11] There is no direct access from man to God, especially if—to refer to Sartre's caustic gloss—not only is the gate made only for each of us, but each of us makes his own gate. We cannot achieve authentic existence self-sufficiently. How, then, are we to achieve it?

Kafka sought it through his writing. Literature became his means of grace, his way of salvation. He wrote in his diaries: "I am more and more unable to think, to observe, to determine the truth of things, to remember, to speak, to share an experience; I am turning to stone, this is the truth. . . . If I can't take refuge in some work, I am lost." "But I will write in spite of everything, absolutely; it is my struggle for self-preservation."[12] Writing he considered as a form of prayer. There is no doubt that his greatest satisfaction, however ephemeral, came from it. Like Flaubert, as Max Brod tells us in his biography, Kafka sacrificed everything to his idol. One thing, however, he could not sacrifice to it, and that was what the God of the Old Testament required of man— a contrite heart. In this light alone can we understand

Kafka's entry for the 25th of September, 1917, in which he declares that he could not be happy unless he succeeded in introducing the world to the true, the pure, the indestructible.

In *The Trial*, Joseph K. sees in a dream the artist Titorelli, who is the official painter of the tribunal and has some definite information concerning the outcome of the trial. Joseph K. asks him what the three possibilities are. Finally, the painter acquiesces and, "having performed a mysterious metamorphosis, he conducts Joseph K. towards his deliverance, and disappears. Art is not salvation."[13] "Art," Kafka wrote, "sacrifices and cancels itself."[14] It cannot name the unnamable. It cannot invent that which is symbolized. Nor could man be happy in imitating God.

But in acknowledging the failure of art, Kafka admits something else, too: his novels are not temples sheltering relics of obsolete symbols, purely and simply. Neither are they some kind of invocation to an unknown God. Rather, they are an unknown man's invocation to God. Or else why should Kafka have written? Obviously, he did not think that faith was something into which man could grow by himself, even if, in *The Castle*, he portrayed the land surveyor K as someone who seeks but one thing, to cease being a stranger, to be admitted into the community, to be accepted.

In "Pourquoi parler" (*Nouvelle Revue Française*, December, 1962), Brice Parain notes that what Western culture is seeking today is perhaps a new religion, a new faith. "But a religion, or a faith, regardless of how greatly the need is felt, one cannot give to oneself." This would contradict the very definition of faith. Only a Messiah can give it. Meanwhile one can only pray. "But in order to pray, one must already have faith," and in whose name shall one pray? The situation thus seems to be without exit, and just at this point we seem to have rejoined Kafka. Or have we? Indeed, we have come to a gate and it is locked. Trying one key after another might occupy us a whole lifetime, but it will not unlock the gate. No cage ever went looking for a bird.[15] "From a certain point onward there is no longer any turning back. That is the point that must be reached."[16]

What is this point of no return? It is the incommensurability between God and man, yes, between God's justice and man's justice; the point of no return lies in the awareness that life cannot be corseted in the straitjacket of logical consistency. From a human point of view, life is the sum total of its contradictions, as Sartre would say. Quite simply, however, Kafka's problem is that of Abraham and that of Job. The only difference consists in the fact that Kafka apprehends his situation in the context not of a transcendental but of an immanentist universe. That probably is the reason God does not come into the picture.

But we must consider a further aspect of Kafka's statement of the problem. Not only is there no common measure between God's justice and man's; from where modern man stands, he can hope to understand God's justice even less than Job did. Accordingly, faith is all the more necessary if man wants to continue assuming responsibility for his existence: besides, "how could one help but go on living?"

Justice is always that of others. It has no common measure with one's own. Man is hence guilty and innocent alike. "We cannot assert the innocence of anyone," writes Camus in *The Fall*, "whereas we can state with certainty the guilt of all."[17] Quite simply, man is guilty precisely because he claims that he is innocent. In a letter to F. B., which he reproduces in his diaries (October 1, 1917), Kafka writes: "Should I examine myself thoroughly in order to know my ultimate goal, I would realize that I do not truly aspire to be good and conform to the exigencies of a supreme Tribunal. . . .One thing alone matters . . . this human tribunal which, besides, I seek to cheat without committing any fraud. . . ."[18] Kafka knows that this sounds like committing a fraud in order to establish one's innocence. In fact, no sooner than begun, such an undertaking demonstrates its own futility by forcing man to face the real nature of the dilemma that splits him in the very heart of his being. On the one hand, "God is not needed to create guilt or to punish. . . . God's sole usefulness would be to guarantee innocence."[19] On the other hand, unable to claim innocence as his own victory, man cannot guarantee his existence either. He fails.

But we have not grasped the full meaning of this failure until we have finally consented to consider it as the failure and crisis of atheism, of innocence attempting to authenticate itself. Existence is not possible, man cannot live unless he is innocent, and if, more significantly, his innocence is guaranteed: man thus fails, but in an ultimate sense he can fail only because of God's absence—or, before God only. The crisis of man without God is thus the crisis of man before God. Once secularized, innocence defeats itself, whereas in the strange solidarity of guilt from which no one is excluded, much less by putting on the mask of innocence, "every man testifies to the crime of all the others."[20] Before whom? Oneself? Obviously this would be ludicrous. Before God, then? We might recall, here, Kafka's relationship with his father. He can assert himself only against his father, but he cannot conceive either rest or happiness without his father.[21]

The fundamental difference between Kafka and the atheist consists in that Kafka never cites God in his stories; he does not take God's name in vain or make graven images. Indeed, one might go so far as to say that Kafka's man almost belies Calvin's understanding of man as an idol-maker. *Almost*: to wit, the father's verdict in the *Judgment* is preceded by this remark: "An innocent child, yes, that you were, truly, but still more truly you have been a devilish human being!—And therefore take note: I sentence you now to death by drowning."[22]

Atheism objects that God is what each one conceives somewhat after his own fashion. By contrast, Kafka's insight is incomparably more perspicacious. No doubt, he sees the validity of the atheist's objection. He even makes it his own. But, while seemingly asserting it himself, he also invalidates it in one stroke by showing that it is a *trompe-l'oeil*. His point is well taken: one cannot use the absence of God in order to justify one's innocence anymore than one can use God to justify one's morality or one's religion. God is no exhibit in man's trial, no mere supporting document of man's case for himself. One cannot justify one's innocence. Nor can one choose to be innocent, any more than one can, as Groethuysen says apropos of *The Trial*, "choose one's own crime."[23] One knows too much to believe in one's innocence, much less to be innocent. To be means to be guilty. Indeed, should he be innocent, man could not bear his condition. Only the devilish, or inauthentic, man would dare make such a claim of innocence: at best, he uses it to hide himself, just as, in other climates and under different auspices, he can parade his religiosity in order better to conceal the face of God.

Clearly, on this point, Kafka's understanding of man's predicament, irrefragably though unexpectedly, quite conforms with biblical thought. Here too, one must add, Kafka does not merely reproduce biblical thought. That would scarcely make sense in a universe the frame of reference of which exhibits qualities that are incongruous with the biblical conception. Though Kafka seems to contradict the latter, he actually reiterates the biblical insight into the nature of man in terms of the only available universe of discourse of all those that are possible—his own, and our, immanentist world view. Indeed, both from Kafka's and the biblical points of view, to be means to be guilty. According to Genesis, the history of man begins with his fall. The state of Adamic innocence is not a human quality per se: it belongs to God, as Karl Barth points out, and not to man.[24] It qualifies man as God's creature. Being the seal of God on his creation, as it were, it signifies God's claim on man and on his allegiance. Accordingly, the notion of fallenness presupposes God's claim on man. Sinfulness implies that man should know why he is guilty, but does not. It means, however, that man claims innocence as his own quality, and that he wants to become like God but turns out to be his own idol. This is exactly the conclusion Kafka reaches by coming from the opposite direction. He writes: "The state in which we find ourselves is sinful, quite independently of guilt."[25]

In the last analysis, innocence comes to signify for Kafka the responsibility we must assume: it is our necessity to be—and to be guilty, for the simple reason that man sets up gods where there is no God and becomes an idolator, that is, a man without God: "The choice was put to them whether they would like to be kings or king's couriers," Kafka writes in his parable of the Couriers. "Like children they all wanted to be couriers. So now there are a great many couriers, they post through the world, and, as there are no kings left, shout to each other their meaningless and obsolete messages. They would gladly put an end to their wretched lives, but they dare not because of their oath of service."[26]

Thus innocence is the incapacity of knowing in the name of whom or of what we may assume such responsibility. "It is a mandate. Because of my very nature I can assume nothing other than a mandate I have received from no one." Neither can he, on the other hand, refuse to accept such a mandate, if only because of his "oath of service." "It is in this contradiction and ever in this contradiction that I can live."[27] In the light of Kafka's logic, what else can this mean than that innocence is the illusion by which self-contradiction attempts to put up with itself, or simply the rationalization of meaninglessness? Besides, to whom is the courier without a king to deliver his meaningless message? Therefore, the innocent is like one who would proclaim his innocence, but there is nobody who listens or even hears what he proclaims in the first place. Innocence cannot be proved, especially if existence is the sum total of its contradictions. Ultimately, the innocent looks like one who would confess his sinfulness—but, he thinks, there is only that which denies him. Or is there?

We have now come to the fundamental implication of Kafka's work. Let us state it gradually. By his very nature man is against God. But he cannot be without him. Neither the claiming of innocence nor atheism—which in effect amounts to the same thing—can resolve this contradiction. As Camus put it, the ultimate attempt of the land surveyor is to find God through that which denies him.[28] But Camus, too, immediately misses the point. What denies God is not his inscrutability or his indifference, nor is it his injustice. What attempts to deny God and fails is man's indifference and man's injustice, just as, on another level, it is equally man's *trompe-l'oeil* religiosity and morality, that is to say, his pretension to deity. The God against whom Kafka rebels, the God who for him is dead, in the last analysis, is not the Wholly Other but that which we mistake for God by writing man in capital letters—the universal hypothesis that serves no other purpose than as a prop to justify our pretenses, our contradictions. No more than it was possible to build the tower of Babel without ascending it, can God be reached by simply assembling our contradictions and pretenses as "a tower with its top in the heavens." Climb as high as we may the scaffolding of our innocence, God is not "its top in the heavens."

What this means is that any tower of Babel, since it must be built by ascending it, makes God unnecessary. This applies to our denial of God as well as to our religious systems: they are the necessary scaffolding that prevents the building of the tower. God cannot be reached or denied if man must climb the scaffolding of self-justification. God is no *tour de force* by which existence may authenticate itself and thus invalidate God. Accordingly, *mutatis mutandis,* in the context of an immanentist universe the atheist faces the same predicament as does the theist in the context of a transcendental universe.

The difference may be expressed in the following manner. The dilemma of the theist is that he takes God for granted and ends by building a tower of Babel. The dilemma of the atheist, on the other hand, lies in that he eliminates God but cannot avoid him. It is the dilemma, furthermore, of the contemporary world. Being immanentist, modern man's world view, so to speak, seeks to dig the pit of Babel. No more than the tower, does it succeed in eliminating God. In other words, God is no longer necessary, he is inevitable.

Would it be too much, from this vantage point, to say that the atheist is the herald of that God who is no longer necessary—no longer the necessary cog of a universal machine, no longer a missing link? Or, to borrow a biblical phrase, the atheist is the herald of the coming God, that God who precisely is no longer necessary in the immanentist framework of our universe. Exactly this, one could legitimately argue, is the point of the question asked in the New Testament: "When the Son of Man comes will he find faith on earth?" As Kafka himself wrote: "The Messiah will come only when he is no longer necessary; he will come only on the day after his arrival; he will come, not on the last day, but on the very last."[29]

Meanwhile, Kafka remarks, life is such a distraction that it prevents us even from realizing what we are distracted from. To be, therefore, is to be guilty. By the same token, existing is itself an act of faith. To live means to believe. To have faith means to be freed from our pretension to dispense with God as well as from our false conceptions of God (as all our conceptions are): "Believing means liberating the indestructible element in oneself, or more accurately, liberating oneself, or more accurately, being indestructible, or more accurately being."[30] Indeed, "man cannot live without an enduring trust in something indestructible in himself. Yet while doing that he may all his life be unaware of that indestructible thing and of that trust in it. One of the possible ways in which this permanent unawareness may be expressed is to have faith in a personal God."[31] Only thus can what we call the way cease from being mere wavering. Hidden or revealed the goal is there. But the ways of man do not lead to it. Something always obstructs them: it is the bush, the same that was burning and yet was not consumed: "The thornbush is the old obstacle in the road. It must catch fire if you want to go further."[32]

We have, indeed, come a long way from Abraham, the father of faith, who put his own faith into question by his willingness to sacrifice Isaac, the child he and Sara had in their old age. But the radical immanentism that informs existence today gives us only the illusion that Abraham's story is improbable, chiefly because God's absence is the only reality we can experience, because he has become unnecessary. But God is inevitable. And man still wishes to imitate Abraham—if only he could be another Abraham. But supposing he could be, he would have no Isaac to sacrifice. To an age for which God is dead, Kafka seems to be saying: if it were possible to believe in God without sacrificing Isaac God would be dead.

V.
Christianity in a Post-Christian Era

****

Le monde est beau, et hors de lui point de salut.

—CAMUS[1]

GOD is man's failure. Never does this become so manifest as in periods of transition, like ours, which are essentially periods of spiritual *interregnum.* Throughout the ages, Christian or not, pre-Christian and post-Christian, God has been man's failure. And in the death of his gods, man both fails and overcomes his failure.

It is not sacrilegious to speak of the death of God, or of God as the chief failure of man. After all, the concept of God is a cultural—not to say ethnolatrous—concept, and God often is nothing other than some sort of constant accessory of culture. Concepts can be valid only so long as they spearhead the spontaneous expression of a particular human experience; they can live only as long as their cultural framework lasts. But a culture is also materialized by institutions, and these tend to overwhelm and atrophy the human experience, until they have invalidated it. By thus defrauding the concept, institutions objectify and ultimately transform into an empirical datum the human reality they are supposed to incarnate.

In the gospel of John, the incarnation means the constantly unique event through which destiny is improvised once and for all, and not its objectification. Human existence, because it can never be rehearsed, is not an institution but a necessary improvisation of destiny. Admittedly, institutions too are born of the necessity of improvisation, but they freeze it, they codify it, just as dogmas and religion betray faith by codifying the acts of faith—through which they are improvised—forgetting that existence itself, as a spontaneous act of faith, is an impertinent improvisation on the theme of God's reality, of the presentness of God.

Unfortunately, organized religion with its variegated paraphernalia, by trying to show how pertinent faith is, blunts it and mummifies it. No improvisation thus lasts beyond the moment when it is conceived, and the concept that results from it leads finally to the institutionalization of religion, or to the cultural annexation of God, or the deliquescence of faith into religiosity. To cite Karl Barth, man can only formulate concepts that are not identical with God; there is no adequacy between God and our concepts of God.[2] Religion and its gods are, consequently, so many screens, so many obstacles between the living God and man. No wonder, according to biblical thought, God in whose image man is created is imageless. And we may, quite appropriately, paraphrase Faulkner's sentence when he writes in *The Sound and the Fury,* "it was men invented virginity, not women,"[3] by saying: it was men invented religion, not God. It was men invented the God that dies.

Indeed, men take pleasure in inventing religions, if not quite to the point of patenting them, at least to that of "incorporating" them. This stricture is not directed against certain American denominations only; every Christian confession is similarly reprehensible whether it is established officially as territorial or unofficially as cultural church, or whether it is incorporated in Vatican State. Christianity itself, as a whole, comes under this judgment insofar as it has *de facto* become the trademark of Western culture.

To speak of the death of God means, then, that finally at the end of the Christian phase of Western culture, the reality of the living God is freed from the cultural concepts and other institutions that attempt to objectify and domesticate it. The death of God marks the end of Christian culture and, especially, of its attempt to assimilate *the other God,* the living God of whom our religion as well as our diffuse religiosity is a desperate caricature. This means that, man being a religious animal, we are groping for a new concept of God and a new attitude, a mode of being congruous with it; that a new religiosity is dawning. And a new era begins when a new religiosity appears, rises from the empty tomb of the dead God.

It was Montesquieu who said, a couple of centuries ago, that Protestantism was bound to disappear, but that, when it has disappeared, Catholicism will have become Protestant. This might well happen. But what will Christianity itself have become by that time? Will it not have fully and plainly become what it already seems to be—nothing more than the bed of a new religiosity, whether this be the threefold religiosity of America's three-religions-and-no-faith, or the cultural, ethnolatrous theology of the West against its rivals for world domination? Montesquieu overlooked the fact that Christianity (ever since it baptized the pagan, syncretistic religiosity of the Mediterranean world) was creating its own religiosity, just as the craving for a drug replaces the illness it was meant to cure. Thalidomide, meant to ease some pains, resulted in "monsters." Christianity "eased the pains" of the world into which the Word was made flesh, but the religious monstrosity it conceived has now become our torment or the object of our disdain.

The dissolution of Christianity into religiosity is what Montesquieu failed to see. (We must not blame him for that. After all, is it not true that we can only wear the face of our religion and that religion can only wear the face of the culture it masks?) Between Montesquieu and ourselves, the death of God has marked this transition from a Christianity resting on the Christianized religiosity of the Roman Empire to our post-Christian religiosity which rests on the ruins of the Christian era.

Thus the death of God has also resulted in the unmasking of the latent, diffuse religiosity to which man is, by nature, inclined. It may well be, therefore, as Mircea Eliade remarks, that the present period will go down in history as the first to have rediscovered "diffuse religious experiences," to have recovered the relevance of raw diffuse religiosity, once overcome by the triumph of Christianity.[4]

But this post-Christian religiosity may also force Christianity out of its Western cage, enable it to break through the walls of Occidentalism and develop into a new historic reality and into a new possibility as individual existence. Doubtless, there are concrete obstacles hindering such expectations for the survival of Christianity. And what if the Christian tradition were checkmated by these obstacles? Such an eventuality is not impossible: it is becoming more and more evident if not absolutely inescapable.

Nonetheless, everything still depends on the ultimate effect of the transition from radical monotheism to radical immanentism and of the leveling down of transcendental values to immanental ones. Either this effect will consist in the recovery of our classic, transcendental categories, according to which God is distinct from, wholly other than his creation. Or else, God has been, so to speak, *renaturalized*, into an immanental force, animating the compulsory ideology of the classless society, at one end of the spectrum, and our most democratic pretensions to deity at the other end. Either way, one thing is clear: man is not an atheist, except by contrast with an established theism, whether it be monotheism or polytheism. As Jean Guitton has said, man is essentially an idolater or an "iconoclast," but not an atheist.[5] But this aspect of the problem cannot concern us at this point, except insofar as it helps us to stress the iconoclastic element peculiarly inherent in the biblical view of existence, or the iconoclastic nature of man's obligation to God.

Our present crisis stems from the fact that we have changed the biblical iconoclasm of the Christian tradition into the idolatrous post-Christian religiosity of our cultural institutions, be they social, political, economic, or ecclesiastical.

And let us not pretend that Christianity has never been *really* tried. It is dishonest to do so after nearly twenty centuries of Christian apologetics, intellectually or ethically, religiously or institutionally as well as culturally. Besides, that same claim could be made for all the dead religions that are now preserved in the religious wax museum of mankind. To pretend that Christianity has never been really tried can only imply, not that its ideals have been much too difficult and demanding for mortal men to realize, but that we are seeking dubious excuses to conceal the fact (as Teilhard de Chardin has rightly observed) that, because Christianity is neither pure nor demanding enough, it can command our allegiance no longer. The death of God is, after all, not a divine failure but the failure of Christian man, like other human failures in history.[6] "Splendid results attained by Christendom!" exclaimed Kierkegaard as he remarked that unfaith, the impossibility or "inability to believe" was now "the sign of a deeper nature."[7]

The repudiation of Christianity does not, of course, entail the repudiation of religion. It does imply, however, that mythological Christianity has given way to a technological religiosity; or that, in Berdyaev's terms, religion used to play a *symbolic* rôle in the shaping of Western culture, but has now become pragmatic and utilitarian. Technological religiosity simply corroborates the increasing irrelevance of Christianity now become the syndrome of the death of God. In plain words, Christianity was regressing even while it brought about the cultural development that presided over the birth of our technological society.

And yet the de-divinization of nature (as necessitated by biblical thought) need not have resulted in the "deconsecration" or secularization of the world. Secularity, or involvement in the world for the sake of God's glory, need not have slipped into secularism. Fostered by Christianity, secularism has been the best expression of the immanentist religiosity that has succeeded the radical monotheism of classical Christianity, when nature, de-divinized, was still conceived of as made for grace. Man's preeminence over the creation was an act of faith. His conquest of the universe is today a technological act of prowess if not simply a technical problem. This deterioration had already set in when in the modern period "reason was cultivated at the expense of spirit."[8] No wonder, then, that today we cultivate religiosity at the expense of faith in God. That is why we can reverse

Kierkegaard's statement and claim that Western culture is the misfortune of Christianity. And that is also why Christianity has remained a Western if not a strictly European phenomenon.

At this point, the question becomes: Can Christianity disentangle itself from the present crisis of Western culture? In other words, is Christianity regressing or developing?

It must be borne in mind that any development of Christianity is by necessity a matter of faith. Unlike economic goals, it will not be achieved through any sort of five-year plan. Insofar as one can distinguish Christianity from its religious and cultural institutions, it is not an empirical datum but the expression of an act of faith. In order to develop, Christianity must, accordingly, dissociate itself from those institutions of Western culture that are catalyzing the present spiritual crisis. And by doing this Christianity would be truly iconoclastic, smashing its own golden calf. To paraphrase St. Vincent of Lerins, the task is to say all things in a new way without proclaiming insidious novelties. The time has come to proclaim the gospel in a new, bold manner, yet without proclaiming a new gospel. Never easy, this kind of task is still more difficult today, and the future quite precarious, what with all the newfangled ideologies that compete with Christianity—and not always unsuccessfully—both at home and abroad.

As we have said, Christianity has until now been almost exclusively a European or Western phenomenon. But the realities of the present world have forced Europe and America to realize that the destiny of the West must include non-Western countries. The era of geographic narcissism has gone—whether that be a good thing or not. The fact is that the ideological gigantism of the modern world and its economic, political, social, religious, and philosophical ramifications will burst through the frame of "European" Christendom, and dislocate Christianity—unless, of course, Christianity should choose to become solely the homegrown religion of the West, for internal use only.

As an empirical datum Christianity has regressed, and this precisely because it has fulfilled itself in Western culture, or, more accurately, in the Christian or Constantinian phase of Western culture. This judgment is based on the claim—I should prefer to say, on the fact —that culturally, if not theologically, there has been a Christian era. Though every age is in need of God's grace and accordingly no age is Christian from a strict theological point of view, the fact remains that our cultural institutions, from the church to our democratic ideals, are unmistakably Christian and not Buddhist or what-have-you; Christianity has become an empirical datum.

We may, therefore, and must, in fact, consider our problem in terms of Christianity in this light. Before inquiring into its three main aspects, *i.e.*, theological, ecclesiastical-institutional, and cultural, let us state our premises. If God is dead, then it follows that as an empirical datum Christianity is regressing. It follows, too, that such a situation makes it culturally impossible to become a Christian under the present circumstances. But it does not follow that no act of faith, no new proclamation of the kerygma (*i.e.*, the core of the gospel) can never take place and overcome this self-invalidation of Christianity.

The future of Christianity depends, in other words, upon a cultural reconversion. This is exactly what I understand Tillich to mean when he writes: "the destruction of the ontological argument is not dangerous. What is dangerous is, the destruction of an approach which elaborates the possibility of the question of God. This approach is the meaning and truth of the ontological argument."[9] With such a statement we are already dealing with the first of the three aspects I have mentioned, the theological.

It is a truism to say that the critical moments of Western history have also involved the greatest theological activity. And there is no self-congratulation—no delusion either—in claiming that in this period of crisis, too, we are witnessing a theological work of such magnitude that it can be advantageously compared with the best examples of the past. From Karl Barth to Father Teilhard, including Tillich and D'Arcy, Niebuhr and Maritain as well as, of course, Rudolf Bultmann, there has emerged a constellation of thinkers who are, as the above quotation from Tillich shows, in no sense lagging behind the times. Nor are they, as some did when Christianity was faring in better circumstances, accommodating the Christian faith to the exigencies of the *Zeitgeist*, even while they cope with them. This is not the place to review their work individually, or to assess the impact of their thought upon contemporary intellectual life. Like the sociologists, we must content ourselves with generalities, and concern ourselves with empirically observable facts.

Let us, then, admit that it would be a sign of intellectual impotence to chide our theologians for any lack of comprehension of our spiritual and philosophical problems. Christian theological activity has seldom been quite so alive. But this activity seems to take place mostly in the areas of Christian existence that are less, if at all, governed by the institutionalism of our ecclesiastical organizations. Indeed, nothing resists so much the institutionalism of Christian confessions as does Barth's *Kirchliche Dogmatik* (ecclesiastical dogmatics). And Teilhard's work is published without the *imprimatur*. There is some irony in pointing out that for the first time we have theologians without churches or theological systems without their corresponding ecclesiastical apparatus.

Without doubt, it is permissible to consider today's theological renewal as a part and preparation or even a precondition of the cultural reconversion without which there can be no further Christian development, no new Christian historical departure. At the same time, one must also point out, it seems, that our Christian institutions have not yet proved themselves worthy of such a magnificent renewal. To put the matter differently and, perhaps, in theologically more accurate terms, it is as if we had arrived at the point where one can still sense in our institutions the presence of the Christian tradition, but it does not coincide with contemporaneous Christian thought. Conversely, the best Christian thinking is today cut off from the tradition as represented by its institutions. Which means, in the words of Isaiah, that

> We have become like those thou hast never ruled,
> like those who are not called by thy name.

The theological evidence thus points to the practical possibility of God's absence. And even stranger is the fact that the reality of God is eclipsed by the very institutions of the Christian tradition.

This brings us to the ecclesiastical-institutional aspect of the problem. Christianity lives on under the form of secularism; for this reason, the demarcation line between regression and development is here almost imperceptible. As a result, most of what is left of Christianity flirts with pluralism, while the rest of it has degenerated into a thoroughgoing syncretism. As Dostoevski said, when the gods lose their indigenous character they die, and so do their people. A few believers, of course, survive, headed against the stream of "churchgoers," those ardent supporters of the perennial institutionism of the Christian churches. But the thing that draws our attention, without surprising us really, is that institutionalism and secularism always seem to go hand in hand. And yet, it is to the sclerotic institutions of Christianity that some have invited us to turn "with some hope," claiming as does Martin Marty that "we already possess the institutions we need to undertake the religious task set before" us.[10] Possibly, a certain degree of hopefulness is permissible, but we should not neglect to use caution, lest these institutions be like the lips with which we honor God while our hearts are far from him. To cite Isaiah again: "because this people draw near with their mouth and honor me with their lips, while their hearts are far from me . . . the wisdom of their wise men shall perish, and the discernment of their discerning men shall be hid."[11]

Peter Berger reminds us that the Church is an article of faith, not an empirical datum. He writes: "Now, it is certainly true that no human culture is so designed as to facilitate conversion. The Jewish culture of Jesus' own time was not so designed. Neither was the Graeco-Roman into which the Christian message was carried by Paul. In other words, the Christian faith will always be in tension with the world. What is characteristic of our situation is that the religious establishment itself obscures this tension and produces the illusion that what tension there is can be understood as growing pains."[12]

Indeed, to be less iconoclastic than those outside the Church would be the greatest treason of Christianity. Nor can one force happiness down other people's throats, let alone faith; and yet this is exactly what our institutions have generally attempted to do. Or over and over again they keep fighting old battles not only in theological matters but also in the spheres of politics and economics—if a battle is engaged in at all. For example, it is doubtful whether the separation of Church and State is a valid theological issue of our time. Our ecclesiastical factions waste their energy, it seems, either when they argue radically in favor of it, or when, casuistically, they defend the principle while at the same time they seek, if they do not actually draw, support from the State for various purposes, such as education. The real problem is what the principle of Church-and-State separation has come to mean today; the fact is that the State no longer needs the Church, being itself a sort of clerical organization that has taken over many responsibilities that used to be ecclesiastical.

Incidentally, let us make it clear, if we must, that none of this is meant to minimize the importance of the Ecumenical Movement or of the worldwide council that is being held at the Vatican. Whether they are any indication that the Christian tradition may yet enjoy a new lease on life depends, of course, on whether they are dominated by the institutionalism of the various Christian confessions they represent. Are they not in fact part of the process toward gigantism so characteristic of our age? To be sure, there is nothing intrinsically evil about gigantism, whether or not it is a necessity of the modern world. But when Christianity sanctions this particular trend, the danger is that it may be doing so for merely social and institutional reasons, for the sake of maintaining its status. Should this be the case, not only the Christian ecumenical concern would be misplaced or misguided; it would serve to accelerate the petrifying grip of institutionalism and sanction the definitive surrender of the Christian tradition.

It is more likely, however, that the leaders of both the World Council of Churches and the Vatican Council have sensed the danger that faces the Christian tradition. In this case, they should also realize that the divisions of Christianity rest, in the last analysis, on a conception of faith and existence that is descriptive of, and dependent on, the world view of the so-called Christian era. That is to say, even granting that these divisions were at one time valid for theological reasons, today they have become purely social and institutional: they have lost their theological justification. Nothing less than a radical about-face, such as, for example, an adjustment of dogmas to the realities of our post-Christian era, would convince us of an unsuspected vitality on the part of the Christian tradition. In a post-Christian era, the sociological divisions of Christianity make no sense. They should not be sanctified, but denounced. True iconoclasm begins with oneself, with the smashing of one's own idols, *i.e.*, of one's superannuated conception of God, of faith and religious allegiance.

We come now to the third aspect of Christianity as an empirical datum, the cultural. Actually, all that has been said so far has been largely determined by this aspect. Instead, then, of a repetitious elaboration, we shall rather try to sharpen our focus, and for that we must be ready for paradoxes.

On the one hand, our cultural incapacity for God stems from the radical immanentism that informs human experience today. On the other hand, we are no less religious today than those of the previous era. Religiosity, in other words, has set in, sometimes merely concealing religious anarchy and sometimes hardly concealed by religious pluralism, under the guise of tolerance. But pluralism is a misnomer. Really, should we not, instead, characterize the present phenomenon and plethora of religious experiences as the subtle expression of henotheism? Doubtless, it is not here a question of national henotheism. The gigantism of the modern world would prevent this. But we may legitimately speak of cultural henotheism, whether it be in terms of the legacy of the Judaeo-Christian tradition to the West, or in terms of a more diffuse reality that actually rests on roughly economic, social, political, or ideological allegiances. Is not denominationalism but a concealed form of the modern version of henotheism—not to mention the latest fad, the tripartite religiosity of democracy?

Clearly, I am not advocating religious bigotry and intolerance. But tolerance need not be syncretistic or lead to that institutional pluralism for which God is a social commodity—as was exemplified in the emperor cult of the dying Roman empire. And like the syncretism of the Graeco-Roman world before the rise of the Christian tradition, in the last analysis pluralism can only be an interlude. It often represents nothing other than the lack of vision on the part of a people that is religiously tired, whose God is dead. Obviously, then, if any hope is left that Christianity might somehow recover certain attributes that will make it again relevant to the future of Western culture, it must first of all substitute new cultural patterns for the old ones with which it is identifying itself without any theological justification. Nothing

less than a cultural renovation of Christian institutions—
and that means a radically new approach to the question of Christianity's cultural embodiment—is necessarily prescribed if any theological renascence is to
have some effect outside the walls of the Church as
well as within.

That is why, as we have already underlined, an iconoclastic reconversion, a cultural revolution is sorely
needed, and all the more urgently because neither institutions nor cultural patterns in general are so "designed as to facilitate conversion" to Christianity, if
they are not, as they seem to be today, so designed as
to make it altogether superfluous. By comparison, a
much easier task, indeed, confronted the early Christians. To begin with, they were not immobilized nor
was their vision obscured by already existing institutions, not to mention the fact that the non-Christian institutions were not only religious but also sacral, at
least supernatural in their significance, while our culture has lost its sacral dimension. It follows, therefore,
that the survival of the Christian tradition is handi-
capped rather than helped by the existence of cultural
structures that are Christian in name only. It was doubtless easier to make the conversion from pre-Christian
to Christian than it is from post-Christian to Christian,
and the reasons for this are obviously not merely chronological, as we have attempted to show in the preceding
theological essays on literature.

The conclusions we have reached may be summarized
in the following manner:

First, in its deepest recesses, Western culture is practically immunized against Christianity. Conversely, there has occurred what we might call a cultural neutralization of the Christian tradition. This means that the once powerful and culturally pregnant symbols of the God-man, of the real presence of God's transcendent immediacy, of communion, are now become words of a forgotten language. Our customs still exhale a Christian flavor, but our hearts are not Christian.[13]

Second, assuming that it was Christianity that began to kill the pagan gods of nature, by de-divinizing nature, until modern science simply confirmed their death, it is possible that, in the last analysis, the death of God means the death of those pagan deities that had somehow survived in the Christian cultural conception of God. Accordingly, the absence of God, as the only divine reality that can be experienced today, may yet enable Christianity further to clarify the biblical concept of God as the Wholly Other, because he is the Creator and not a natural force.

Third, the era of Western religious narcissism is gone, and this certainly, is a significant contribution of our post-Christian era to the Christian tradition. The national egotism of emergent countries will perhaps force Christianity to become more kerygmatic at home as well as abroad, that is to say, to help bring about or to awaken us to the need for a cultural renovation by becoming iconoclastic again and, thus, relevant to the culture of the West.

Fourth, the exposing of religious obscurantism and

the absence of supernatural crutches may equally force us to formulate what Berdyaev refers to as our "cultural will," whether as Christians or not, but certainly not as pseudo-Christian Westerners or as pseudo-Western Christians.

Our final point will be made by way of a question borrowed from Saint Augustine: "How could the City of God," he asked, "... either take a beginning or be developed, or attain its proper destiny, if the life of the saints were not a social life?"[14] How can the Christian tradition survive or develop without a concomitant, congruous, cultural reality manifest in all realms of the spirit from theology to art and literature as well as on all levels of life from morality to economics and politics?

In short, the Christian tradition has been regressing insofar as it has not been relevant to the present crisis of our cultural situation. On the other hand, Christian thought has been developing, but it is no longer relevant to the situation of our post-Christian age and its cultural postulates—nor will it be relevant as long as it is tied down by its institutions and by the dogmas of a forgotten language. And should Christianity perchance survive the dishabilitation of its institutions, the least that still must be said is that Western culture is not "ready" for it, as the pre-Christian world once was ready for the Christian gospel.

References

****

PREFACE

1. Paul Tillich, cited from memory.
2. Erich Auerbach, *Mimesis* (Garden City, N. Y., 1957), pp. 64, 490.

I. *Iconoclasm and Transfiguration*

1. Saint Paul, I Corinthians 11/7 (K.J.); II Corinthians 3/17–18 (N.E.B.).

CHRISTIANITY AS ICONOCLASM

1. Heinrich Pestalozzi, quoted by Wilhelm Vischer.
2. Wilhelm Vischer, *La Loi* (Neuchâtel et Paris, 1949), p. 90.
3. André Gide, as reported in *Les Protestants et l'esthétique* (Paris, Le Semeur, 1949).
4. Charles Baudelaire, *The Flowers of Evil* (New York, 1955), p. 168.
5. Baudelaire, *op. cit.*, p. 149.
6. H. Richard Niebuhr, *Radical Monotheism and Western Culture* (New York, 1960), p. 52.
7. Reinhold Niebuhr, *The Children of Light and the Children of Darkness* (New York, 1947), pp. 118, xi.
8. W. H. Auden, *New Year Letter* (London, 1941), lines 1632 ff.

THE NEED FOR A CULTURAL REVOLUTION

1. Sören Kierkegaard, *The Sickness Unto Death* (Garden City, N. Y., 1954), p. 248.
2. Rudolf Bultmann, "New Testament and Mythology" in Hans Werner Bartsch (ed.), *Kerygma and Myth* (New York, 1961), pp. 1–44; *Jesus Christ and Mythology* (New York, 1958), Ch. III.
3. T. S. Eliot, "The Rock," *Collected Poems* (New York, 1936), p. 200.
4. Psalm 137/1–4 (R.S.V.).
5. Jean-Paul Sartre, "La Temporalité chez Faulkner" *Situations I* (Paris, 1947), p. 80.
6. Helen Gardner, *The Art of T. S. Eliot* (New York, 1950), p. 62, n. 1.

7. T. S. Eliot, *On Poetry and Poets* (New York, 1957), pp. 15–16.
8. Samuel Beckett, *Waiting for Godot* (New York, 1954), p. 8.
9. Max Weber, quoted by Eric Voegelin.
10. Eric Voegelin, *The New Science of Politics* (Chicago, 1952), p. 22.
11. Karl Jaspers, *Man in the Modern Age* (New York, 1957), p. 86.
12. Walter Stace, *Religion and the Modern Mind* (Philadelphia, 1960), pp. 93–94.
13. Paul Ricoeur, *Finitude et culpabilité* (Paris, 1960), Vol. II, p. 325.
14. Psalm 139/7–8 (K.J.).
15. Luke 18/8 (N.E.B.).

II. *Between History and the Eternal*

1. John Donne, *The Complete Poetry and Selected Prose of John Donne* (New York, 1952), p. 446.

NATHANIEL HAWTHORNE

1. Hawthorne, "The Birthmark," *Hawthorne's Short Stories*, Newton Arvin (Ed.) (New York, 1955), p. 147.
2. Hawthorne, "Rappaccini's Daughter," *ibid.*, p. 206.
3. Hawthorne, "The Birthmark," *ibid.*, p. 151.
4. *Ibid.*, p. 152.
5. *Ibid.*, p. 158.
6. *Ibid.*, p. 158.
7. *Ibid.*, p. 159.
8. *Ibid.*, pp. 163–164.
9. Hawthorne, *The Scarlet Letter* (New York, 1950), p. 83.
10. *Ibid.*, p. 224.
11. *Ibid.*, p. 297.
12. *Ibid.*, p. 62.
13. *Ibid.*, pp. 126–127.
14. *Ibid.*, p. 138.
15. *Ibid.*, p. 60.
16. St. Augustine, *Confessions*, IV/XV.
17. *The Scarlet Letter*, p. 297.
18. *Ibid.*, p. 53.
19. George Ferguson, *Signs and Symbols in Christian Art* (New York, 1961), p. 37.

20. *The Scarlet Letter*, pp. 125–126.
21. *Ibid.*, p. 107.
22. *Ibid.*, p. 110.
23. *Ibid.*, p. 154.

HERMAN MELVILLE

 1. Melville, *Moby Dick* (New York, 1950), pp. 27, 49.
 2. *Ibid.*, p. 49.
 3. *Ibid.*, p. 51.
 4. *Ibid.*, p. 54.
 5. *Ibid.*, p. 3.
 6. *Ibid.*, p. 36.
 7. *Ibid.*, p. 36.
 8. *Ibid.*, p. 36.
 9. *Ibid.*, p. 39.
10. *Ibid.*, p. 47.
11. *Ibid.*, p. 48.
12. *Ibid.*, p. 80.
13. *Ibid.*, p. 56.
14. *Ibid.*, p. 61.
15. *Ibid.*, p. 552.
16. *Ibid.*, p. 428.
17. *Ibid.*, p. 428.
18. *Ibid.*, pp. 47–48.
19. *Ibid.*, p. 428.
20. Karl Jaspers, *Philosophie* (Berlin, 1932), vol. III, p. 229; quoted by P. Tillich, *Theology of Culture* (New York, 1959), p. 97.
21. Melville, *op. cit.*, p. 225.

WILLIAM FAULKNER

1. Faulkner, *The Sound and the Fury* and *As I Lay Dying* (New York, 1946), p. 299.
2. André Malraux, "Préface à *Sanctuaire*," *Nouvelle Revue Française CCXLII*, p. 744 (Paris, 1933).
3. *The Sound and the Fury*, p. 63.
4. Gabriel Marcel, *Homo Viator* (Paris, 1944), p. 71.
5. *The Sound and the Fury*, p. 16.
6. *Ibid.*, p. 10.
7. *Ibid.*, p. 16.
8. *Ibid.*, p. 16.

9. *Ibid.*, p. 199.

10. *Ibid.*, p. 301.

11. *Ibid.*, p. 113.

12. *Ibid.*, p. 306.

13. *Ibid.*, p. 250.

14. *Ibid.*, p. 292.

15. *Ibid.*, p. 77.

16. Claude-Edmonde Magny, *L'Age du roman américain* (Paris, 1948), p. 210.

17. Jean-Paul Sartre, *op. cit.*

18. *The Sound and the Fury*, p. 123.

19. *Ibid.*, p. 192.

20. Jean-Paul Sartre, *Being and Nothingness* (New York, 1956) [*L'Etre et le Néant* (Paris, 1943), pp. 71, 97, 108, 132, 713.]

21. *The Sound and the Fury*, p. 197.

22. *Ibid.*, p. 95.

23. *Ibid.*, p. 104.

24. *Ibid.*, p. 108.

25. *Ibid.*, pp. 312–313.

26. *Ibid.*, p. 313.

27. Rudolf Bultmann, *New Testament Theology* (New York, 1955), II, p. 77.

28. *Ibid.*, p. 89.

29. *The Sound and the Fury*, p. 309.

30. *John*, I, 46.

31. *The Sound and the Fury*, p. 309.

32. *Ibid.*, p. 298.

33. *Ibid.*, p. 44.

34. Albert Camus, *The Myth of Sisyphus* (New York, 1959), p. 64.

35. Faulkner, "Black Music," *Collected Stories of William Faulkner* (New York, 1950), p. 809.

III. *The Best Possible World*

1. Rainer Maria Rilke, *Die Sonette an Orpheus* (Paris, 1943), I/III.

T. S. ELIOT

1. Gabriel Vahanian, *The Death of God* (New York, 1961), p. 60 ff. and *passim*.

2. Karl Barth, *Der Roemerbrief* (Berne, 1919; Munich, 1920, 1922).

3. Quoted by David Daiches, *Poetry and the Modern Mind* (Chicago, 1940), p. 94.

4. F. O. Matthiessen, *The Achievement of T. S. Eliot* (New York, 1947), pp. 144–145.

5. *Ibid.*, p. 145.

6. Eliot, *After Strange Gods* (New York, 1934), p. 45.

7. R. A. Scott-Jones, *Fifty Years of English Literature, 1900–1950* (London, 1951), p. 161.

8. Eliot, *The Cocktail Party* (New York, 1950), p. 144.

9. Eliot, *The Confidential Clerk* (New York, 1954), p. 154.

10. Eliot, *Selected Essays* (New York, 1950), p. 17.

11. Eliot, "The Waste Land," *Collected Poems 1909–1935* (New York, 1936), lines 423 ff.

12. *Ibid.*, lines 131 ff.

13. St. John of the Cross, epigraph to "Sweeney Agonistes," *Collected Poems*, p. 135.

14. Eliot, *Selected Essays*, pp. 328–329.

15. *Ibid.*, p. 300.

16. *Ibid.*, p. 342.

17. Eliot, *Murder in the Cathedral* (New York, 1935), p. 44.

18. Eliot, "The Waste Land," *op. cit.*, lines 388 ff.

19. Eliot, "The Rock," *Collected Poems*, p. 204.

20. Eliot, "Ash Wednesday," *ibid.*, p. 118.

21. "The Rock," *ibid.*, p. 192.

22. Eliot, *Four Quartets* (New York, 1943), p. 17.

23. Eliot, "The Rock," *op. cit.*, p. 181 f.

24. Eliot, "The Waste Land," *op. cit.*, lines 418 ff.

25. Eliot, "Journey of the Magi," *Collected Poems*, p. 126.

26. Eliot, *Notes Towards the Definition of Culture* (New York, 1949), p. 32.

27. *Ibid.*, p. 32.

28. Ludwig Feuerbach, *The Essence of Christianity*, with an introductory essay by Karl Barth (New York, 1957), p. xiv.

29. Eliot, *Four Quartets*, p. 24.

W. H. AUDEN

1. Auden, *Collected Poetry* (New York, 1945), p. 372.

2. *Ibid.*, p. 420.

3. Auden, *The Shield of Achilles* (New York, 1955), pp. 63–64.

4. "Criticism in a Mass Society," in D. A. Stauffer, ed., *The*

Intent of the Critic (Princeton, 1941), p. 114; cf. also, "The American Scene," *Horizon*, No. 86, p. 87.

5. Auden, "For the Time Being," *Collected Poetry*, p. 420.
6. Auden, *The Age of Anxiety* (New York, 1947), p. 135.
7. *Ibid.*, pp. 137–138.
8. Auden, *Collected Poetry*, p. 198.
9. Auden, "Depravity: A Sermon," *Collected Poetry*, p. 247.
10. Auden, *Collected Poetry*, p. 51.
11. *Ibid.*, p. 447.
12. *Ibid.*, p. 447.
13. *Ibid.*, p. 451.
14. Stephen Spender, *The Destructive Element* (Boston, *The Atlantic*, July, 1953), p. 75.
15. Auden, "Romantic or Free" (Northampton, *Smith Alumnae Quarterly Review*, August, 1940), p. 557.
16. Auden, *Collected Poetry*, p. 413.
17. *Ibid.*, p. 435.
18. *Ibid.*, p. 412.
19. *Ibid.*, p. 416.
20. Auden, *Poems* (New York, 1934), p. 42.

SAINT-JOHN PERSE

1. André Malraux, *The Voices of Silence* (New York, 1953), p. 496.
2. Perse, *Exile and Other Poems* (New York, 1949), pp. 13–15.
3. Georges Bernanos, *The Diary of a Country Priest* (Garden City, 1954), p. 159.
4. Perse, *Eloges and Other Poems* (New York, 1956), p. 5.
5. Perse, *Winds* (New York, 1961), p. 37.
6. Perse, *Exile* (New York, 1949), p. 23.
7. Perse, *Eloges* (New York, 1956), p. 91.
8. *Ibid.*, p. 29.
9. Perse, *Exile*, p. 67.
10. *Ibid.*, p. 89.
11. Perse, *Anabasis* (New York, 1949), p. 29.
12. Perse, *Winds*, p. 167.
13. *Ibid.*, p. 119.

IV. *Faith, Reason and Existence*

1. La Rochefoucauld, *Maximes et réflexions morales* (Paris, 1942), 42.

2. Kierkegaard, *Fear and Trembling* (Garden City, 1954), p. 64.

FYODOR DOSTOEVSKI

1. André Gide, *Dostoievski* (Paris, 1923), p. 70.
2. Dostoevski, *The Brothers Karamazov* (New York, Modern Library Edition), pp. 78, 79, 93. Paul Ramsey, *Nine Modern Moralists* (Englewood-Cliffs, 1962), p. 11 ff.
3. Dostoevski, *op. cit.*, p. 17.
4. *Ibid.*, p. 24.
5. *Ibid.*, p. 170.
6. *Ibid.*, pp. 423–424.
7. *Ibid.*, p. 93.
8. *Ibid.*, p. 78.
9. *Ibid.*, p. 289.
10. *Ibid.*, p. 25.
11. *Ibid.*, p. 291.
12. *Ibid.*, p. 93.
13. *Ibid.*, pp. 288, 289.
14. *Ibid.*, p. 291.
15. Edward Thurneysen, *Dostoievski ou Les confins de l'homme* (Paris, 1934).
16. Dostoevski, quoted by Gide, *op. cit.*, pp. 47–48.
17. Nicholas Berdyaev, *Dostoevsky* (New York, 1957), p. 147.
18. Walter Kaufmann, *Religion from Tolstoy to Camus* (New York, 1961), pp. 8–12.
19. Montesquieu, *Cahiers* (Paris, 1951), p. 113.
20. *The Brothers Karamazov*, p. 302.
21. *Ibid.*, p. 303.
22. *Ibid.*, p. 301.
23. *Ibid.*, p. 301.
24. *Ibid.*, p. 796.
25. Thurneysen, *op. cit.*, p. 18.

PAR LAGERKVIST

1. Lagerkvist, *The Dwarf* (London, 1953), pp. 38–39.
2. *Ibid.*, 14.
3. Lagerkvist, *Barabbas* (New York, 1951).
4. *Ibid.*, pp. 179–180.
5. André Gide, in Lagerkvist, *Barabbas*, p. xii.
6. Cf. Psalm 139.

7. Karl Jaspers, *Way to Wisdom* (New Haven, 1960), p. 51.
8. Lagerkvist, *The Sibyl* (New York, 1958), p. 24.
9. *Ibid.*, p. 136.
10. *Ibid.*, p. 151.
11. *Ibid.*, pp. 151–152.

FRANZ KAFKA

1. Kafka, *Parables* (New York, 1947), p. 79.
2. Max Brod, *Franz Kafka* (Berlin & Frankfurt-am-Main, 1954), pp. 68–69.
3. *Ibid.*, p. 65.
4. Jean Starobinski, introduction to *La Colonie pénitentiaire* (Paris, 1945), pp. 29–30.
5. Kafka, "Reflections," in *The Great Wall of China* (New York, 1946), p. 307.
6. Albert Camus, "Remarque sur la révolte," in *L'Existence* (Paris, 1945), p. 15.
7. Kafka, "Fragments," in *Dearest Father* (New York, 1954), p. 349.
8. "Reflections," *op. cit.*, p. 282.
9. *Ibid.*, p. 284.
10. *Ibid.*, p. 283.
11. Kafka, "Before the Law," *The Penal Colony, Stories and Short Pieces* (New York, 1948), p. 150; *The Trial* (New York, Mod. Lib.), p. 269.
12. Quoted by J. H. Miller in *The Tragic Vision and the Christian Faith*, Nathan Scott, ed. (New York, 1957), p. 292.
13. Marthe Robert, *Kafka* (Paris, 1960), p. 66.
14. Kafka, "Eight Octavo Notebooks," in *Dearest Father*, p. 154.
15. "Reflections," *op. cit.*, p. 281.
16. *Ibid.*, p. 279.
17. Camus, *The Fall* (New York, 1957), p. 110.
18. Marthe Robert, *Kafka*, p. 178.
19. Camus, *The Fall*, pp. 110, 111.
20. *Ibid.*, p. 110.
21. Cf. Claude Mauriac, *The New Literature* (New York, 1959). *L'Alittérature contemporaine* (Paris, 1958), p. 24.
22. Kafka, "Judgment," *Selected Stories of Franz Kafka* (New York, 1952, Mod. Lib.), p. 18.

23. Bernard Groethuysen, "A propos de Kafka," in Kafka, *Le Procès* (Paris, 1948), p. 7.
24. Karl Barth, *Kirchliche Dogmatik* (Zollikon-Zürich, 1945), III/I, pp. 351–352; cf. Henri Bouillard, *Karl Barth* (Paris, 1957), II, p. 201, n. 1.
25. Kafka, "Reflections," *op. cit.*, p. 79.
26. *Ibid.*, p. 289; *Parables*, p. 117.
27. Kafka, *Journal intime* (Paris, 1945), p. 222.
28. Camus, *Le Mythe de Sisyphe* (Paris, 1942), p. 181.
29. *Parables*, p. 65. Also, "The Eight Octavo Notebooks," *op. cit.*, p. 78.
30. "The Eight Octavo Notebooks," *op. cit.*, p. 78.
31. "Reflections," *op. cit.*, pp. 52–53.
32. "The Eight Octavo Notebooks," *op. cit.*, p. 75.

V. *Christianity in a Post-Christian Era*

1. Albert Camus, *Noces* (nouvelle édition, copyright Edmond Charlot, 1939), p. 117.
2. Karl Barth, *Fides quaerens intellectum: Anselms Beweis der Existenz Gottes* (Muenchen, 1931), ch. I/3.
3. William Faulkner, *The Sound and the Fury* (New York, Mod. Lib.), p. 97.
4. Mircea Eliade, "Note pour un humanisme," *Nouvelle Revue Française* (Paris, November, 1961).
5. Cf. Henri Fesquet, *Le Catholicisme, religion de demain* (Paris, 1962), p. 105.
6. Nicholas Berdyaev, *Le sens de l'histoire* (Paris, 1948), pp. 182 ff.
7. Kierkegaard, *The Sickness Unto Death* (New York, Anchor Books), p. 246.
8. Wilhelm Röpke, *Die Gesellschaftskrisis der Gegenwart* (Erlenbach-Zürich, 1942), pp. 24–25.
9. Paul Tillich, *Systematic Theology* (Chicago, 1951), V. I, p. 208.
10. Martin Marty, *The New Shape of American Religion* (New York, 1959), p. 122.
11. Isaiah, 29/13–14; Mark 7/6–7. (R.S.V.).
12. Peter Berger, *The Noise of Solemn Assemblies* (Garden City, 1961), p. 117.
13. Alain, *Propos sur la religion* (Paris, 1957), p. 41.
14. St. Augustine, *De civitate dei*, 19/5.